D1209119

A Guide to Programmed Instruction

A Guide to

John Wiley and Sons, Inc.

New York • London • Sydney

Programmed Instruction

Jerome P. Lysaught

Clarence M. Williams

College of Education, University of Rochester

SECOND CORRECTED PRINTING, MAY, 1968

Library of Congress Catalog Card Number: 63:11440
Printed in the United States of America

To Dolores and Mary Lou

Preface

Shortly after this century passed the half-way mark, followers of educational research and industrial training began to observe a new educational star. At first sight, it seemed entirely new; actually, it was nothing of the sort. What drew attention was a novel method of learning that had emerged logically from teaching processes evolving since the glorious days of Greece–and perhaps before. This method was *programmed learning,* and it was beginning to come of age. To those whose mission was to direct others to knowledge, its potentiality was much too promising to be ignored.

Many of those engaged in the instruction of their fellow men responded to the opportunities that programmed learning afforded, among them the authors of this book. Prodded by our professional and personal curiosity, each of us began on his own to develop by trial and error programs of teaching materials built on this newest pedagogical technique. As each–one a professor interested in educational research and the other a specialist in industrial training–faced the necessity of instructing graduate students, teachers, or industrial trainers to construct such programs, he refined his initial procedure and perfected the attitudes, skills, and body of knowledge that would prove helpful to those wishing to program materials for learning. Eventually we fused our individual experiences into one cooperative effort.

Out of this venture came what we believe was the first college course presented in the field of programmed learning. Introduced in January, 1961, at the University of Rochester, the course was improved subsequently as a result of our exposure to other courses, workshops, and seminars in programming, and our receipt of comment and information from former students. In the fall of 1961, the University added an advanced course in programming to cope with supplementary matters of revision, practical application, and the acquisition and analysis of program material.

Conducting both courses has taught us many lessons. Time and again, we have had to back and fill, adjusting the substance of the courses to classroom needs. The relative newness of the discipline and the paucity of printed aids persuaded us that others might be spared the pitfalls that we encountered if the knowledge thus obtained were put between the covers of a book.

This book, then, is intended to serve as a guide to programmed material. It is the first of its kind, a complete blueprint of the techniques of programming. Whether the reader plans to devise models of his own or to use the handiwork prepared by others, this book will familiarize him with the origins and fundamentals of the new method. It will, moreover, teach him to create and evaluate programmed matter in different subject areas, and to use programming for general and specialized educational purposes.

We maintain that no teacher should introduce programmed material into the classroom before he has become well acquainted with the new method and feels at ease with it. Once he has absorbed the basic principles, he is sure to become a better teacher for the knowledge.

Although we have attempted to present a concise guide to the preparation of instructional programs, no single guide can substitute for the actual experience of writing, testing, and revising a learning program. Those who wish to gain the full benefit of this book actually should prepare a programmed unit on the basis of the designs it suggests.

As a final word of introduction, a comment is necessary about the footnotes and references auxiliary to the text. Two valuable books exist in the field. They are *Automatic Teaching: The State of the Art,* edited by Eugene Galanter (Wiley), and *Teaching Machines and Programmed Learning,* edited by A. A. Lumsdaine and Robert Glaser (National Educational Association). Both books contain collections of early papers and articles not readily accessible. Because of this, we have added to each footnote or reference a code indicating whether those papers are available in either Galanter or Lumsdaine and Glaser, and we wish to acknowledge here the assistance those publications have provided.

Programmed learning is still in the exhilarating stages of early experiments and the first flush of primary applications. If this book aids teachers and training specialists to share in the excitement of exploration, it will have fulfilled its aim. We solicit the comments, criticisms, and experiences of readers, while expressing gratitude to former students who so generously contributed their time and energies. For any shortcomings of the book, we alone bear the responsibility.

JEROME P. LYSAUGHT
CLARENCE M. WILLIAMS

Rochester, New York
December 1962

Contents

1 Origins and Fundamentals of Programming 1

2 Selecting a Unit to Be Programmed 29

3 Assumptions about Learners 42

4 Appropriate Objectives 52

5 Selection of a Paradigm 70

6 Constructing the Program 92

7 Editing and Review 119

8 Evaluation 134

9 Applications and Implications 148

Selected Bibliography 168

Index 180

Chapter

One

Origins and Fundamentals of Programming

In the Blue Ridge mountain city of Roanoke, Virginia, pupils in the eighth grade of the local schools in a single term all completed a full year of algebra, normally reserved for the first year of high school in other parts of the country, and only one child in the entire Roanoke school system failed to perform satisfactorily on a standardized examination.[1] At Hamilton College, Clinton, New York, nobody fails the logic course any more; moreover, the average of grades has risen markedly. At the Collegiate School, New York City, a private elementary and secondary institution for boys that long has maintained high scholastic standards, students are now progressing more rapidly in modern mathematics than ever before. These diverse achievements are neither accidents nor as unrelated as a casual reading might suggest. Through them runs a common element. In each instance classroom teachers have been utilizing the techniques of programmed learning, a method of pedagogy that increases the learning rate and proficiency of pupils and students.

The results of these and similar successful experiences are not conclusive, but they have alerted educators at all levels and in many areas of knowledge to a new educational potential. Al-

[1] Rushton, E. W., "Programmed Learning in the Roanoke, Virginia, City School System," unpublished paper dated January 30, 1961. (See also *TEMAC Programmed Learning Materials, Report No. 2,* Wilmette, Ill.: Encyclopaedia Britannica Films, April, 1961.)

though these trials do not represent finely controlled experiments, they contain enough promise to fan interest in the practices that produced them. The learning program, which is the cause of it all, has become more than an object of educational curiosity. In many schools and institutions of higher learning, it is part of the regular teaching repertoire. As reliance on such programs grows, teachers and educators need to know the anatomy of learning programs and the several ways of putting them together.

No doubt before setting forth to organize a learning program one would do well to discover what a learning program is. *Programming* is the process of arranging materials to be learned in a series of small steps designed to lead a student through self-instruction from what he knows to the unknown of new and more complex knowledge and principles. The student responds at each step; when his response is correct he may proceed to the next one. It is rather like an old-fashioned treasure hunt, but one in which the clues are so set out that each hunter will find the reward. The *learning program* is the completed route to mastery of the subject for which it has been prepared—ordered and ready for the student to follow.

Presumably, all teachers desire to guide their students from the familiar to the unfamiliar, and thus to impart knowledge and understanding. In the minds of many, unfortunately, there is an inseparable linking of programmed material with a mechanical *teaching machine*. The teaching machine, however, is simply any device that puts a learning program before a student. It includes any of several forms of text known as a programmed book, and only in a narrower sense does it refer to a mechanical, electrical, or electronic instrument specifically built to present programmed matter to students.

In the new vocabulary inspired by programming, two phrases have gained increasing currency. *Auto-instructional methods* pertain to the complete affair, the process of program construction, the presentation by machine, and the student's activity as he learns from the procedure. *Auto-instructional device* applies to the various types of instruments.*

* The novelty of these terms has given rise to some of the lighter moments in the lives of programming's pioneers. One school administrator inquired

The Beginnings

That great sage of the diamond, Casey Stengel, once remarked after trying to teach one of his young charges a subtle point of the game, "He thinks I was born 60 years old." We sometimes see events, as well as persons, not as growing, unfolding phenomena, but as full blown and fortuitous. Programming is regarded often as a recent development because its practical application to education has become apparent only in the past few years. This may be a flattering comment on the present generation, but unfortunately it is not true. To maintain that programming is a twentieth-century accomplishment is to ignore the emergence of the present form from processes that have evolved down through the ages and to forget the contributions of scholars dating back more than 2000 years.

One of the earliest programmers was Socrates, who developed a program for geometry, which was recorded by Plato in the dialogue, *Meno*. It was Socrates' habit to guide his followers to knowledge by conducting them conversationally along a path from fact to fact and insight to insight. The similarity between his method and the contemporary use of programming is easy to observe. Table 1-1 shows a portion of the Meno compared with a sequence of a modern program.

Closer to our own times has come the tutorial method. This was perfected by the colleges of the great English universities and taken up by many of this country's colleges in one form or another. The continuous exchange of questions and answers between the tutor and his student, the unfolding of information and explanations, and the constant selection of new material on the basis of the student's mastery of what has gone before is indeed a forerunner of programmed instruction.

The antecedents of current programming practices could be explored indefinitely, but that is not the purpose of this book.

about a nearby university's workshop on driver training. The university disclaimed knowledge of any such project, but the administrator persisted; its announcement spoke clearly, he said, of a Workshop on Auto-Instruction. The university immediately dropped the term in favor of programmed learning.

Table 1-1 A Comparison of Items from Two Developmental Instructional Sequences.[2]

Stimulus	
S-1. Then here we have four equal squares? 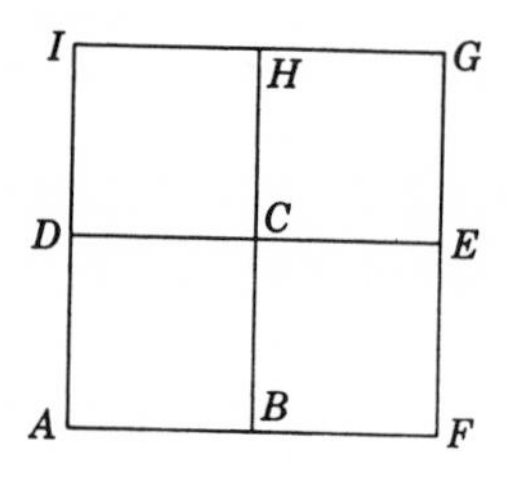	S-1. A doctor taps your knee with a rubber hammer to test your "__________."
	Response
R-1. Yes.	R-1. reflexes
S-2. How many times the size of the first square (*ABCD*) is the whole (*AFGI*)?	S-2. If your reflexes are normal, your leg __________ to the tap on the knee with slight kick.
R-2. Four times.	R-2. responds (or reacts)
S-3. We want one double the size. Now does this line going from corner to corner cut each of the squares in half? 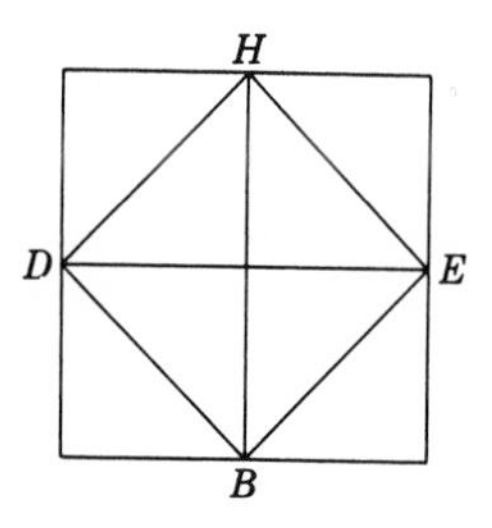	S-3. In the knee jerk or patellar tendon reflex, the kick of the leg is the __________ to the tap on the knee.
R-3. Yes.	R-3. response (or reaction)
S-4. And these are four equal lines enclosing this area? (*BEHD*) (*See S-3 figure.*)	S-4. The stimulating *object* used by the doctor to elicit a knee jerk is a(n) __________.
R-4. Yes.	R-4. hammer (mallet)

[2] Adapted from Guthrie, W. K. C., *Plato, Protagoras and Meno*, Baltimore, Md.: Penguin, 1956, p. 104, and from James F. Holland and B. F. Skinner, *The Analysis of Behavior*, New York: McGraw-Hill, 1961, pp. 2–4.

S-5. Look at our four squares. Has not each line cut off the inner half of each of them?
(*See S-3.*)

R-5. Yes.

S-6. And how many halves are there in this figure? (*BEHD*)
(*See S-3.*)

R-6. Four.

S-7. Right. And how many halves are there in this figure?
(*ABCD*)
(*See S-1.*)

R-7. Two.

S-8. And what is the relation of four to two?

R-8. Double.

S-5. The *stimulus* which elicits a knee jerk is the ________ delivered by the so-called stimulus object or hammer.

R-5. tap (blow)

S-6. In the knee-jerk reflex, we call the rubber hammer the ________ and the tap or blow the ________.

R-6. a. stimulus object
b. stimulus

S-7. An event is explained when its cause is identified. The "cause" or explanation of the knee jerk is, technically, the ________ which elicits it.

R-7. stimulus

S-8. Technically speaking, a reflex involves an eliciting stimulus in a process called elicitation. A stimulus ________ a response.

R-8. elicits

It is clear that the origins of programming are not essentially new; nevertheless, the method as it is now employed may be considered to derive from dynamic efforts begun in the 1920's.

In 1926, Sidney L. Pressey, an Ohio State University psychologist, made public his pioneer studies on the first recognized teaching machine.[3] Pressey's model originally was conceived as a *testing* machine that presented a series of questions to a student and informed him immediately whether his reply was right or wrong. In most respects Pressey's machine had the same capabilities as the machines now in use. Yet despite the promise of his

[3] Pressey, S. L., "A Simple Apparatus Which Gives Tests and Scores—and Teaches," *School and Society,* Vol. 23, No. 586, March 20, 1926 (Lumsdaine and Glaser, pp. 35–41).

experimental results and his interest, along with others,[4–6] in encouraging further research, the movement in behalf of such devices lost its impetus. There are at least two explanations for this. First, no provision was made for systematic programming of materials to be used in these machines, and, second, the onset of the depression and its impact on social conditions and education offered an unfavorable environment for an "industrial revolution" in the nation's schools.

By 1954, however, conditions in the world had changed. Greater knowledge in the science of behavior, especially about the analysis of learning behavior, and a demand for education on an unprecedented scale that strained every educational resource, created a vastly different set of circumstances. In this fresher climate, two Harvard psychologists, B. F. Skinner and James G. Holland, devised auto-instructional methods which have served the current generation as the bases for its own excursions into programmed learning.

The Reinforcement Theory of Learning

At the heart of any learning program lies the practice of what Skinner calls *reinforcement.* There is acknowledgement or reward of some kind to show that an organism has performed to satisfaction. "Once we have arranged the particular type of consequence called a reinforcement," wrote Skinner in 1954, "our techniques permit us to shape the behavior of an organism almost at will."[7] Food and water supplied as reinforcers to lower animals can produce learning patterns among them, as can *conditioned* reinforcers such as tokens which can be exchanged

[4] Pressey, S. L., "A Third and Fourth Contribution Toward the Coming 'Industrial Revolution' in Education," *School and Society,* Vol. 36, No. 934, November 19, 1932 (Lumsdaine and Glaser, p. 47).

[5] Peterson, J. C., "The Value of Guidance in Reading for Information," *Trans. of the Kans. Acad. of Sci.,* Vol. 34, 1931 (Lumsdaine and Glaser, p. 52).

[6] Little, James K., "Results of Use of Machines for Testing and for Drill upon Learning in Educational Psychology," *Journ. of Exper. Educ.,* Vol. 3, 1934 (Lumsdaine and Glaser, p. 59).

[7] Skinner, B. F., "The Science of Learning and the Art of Teaching," *Harvard Educ. Rev.,* Vol. 24, No. 2, 1954 (Lumsdaine and Glaser, p. 100).

for sweets. Among human students, food, money, grades, gold stars, or merely the knowledge of being "right" all serve as reinforcers. Programmed learning has emphasized this final type of reinforcement; it reinforces the learner primarily by acquainting him with the correctness of his learning effort.

Reinforcement theory has sprung from laboratory observation and analysis of the learning behaviors of lower organisms. Nevertheless, a projection of its conclusions to human beings provides new insight into the educational problems of teachers and psychologists alike. These are some generalizations arising from the theory as they pertain to programmed learning: [8]

1. An individual learns or changes the way he acts by observing the consequences of his actions.
2. Consequences that strengthen the likelihood of repetition of an act are called reinforcements.
3. The more quickly reinforcement follows the desired performance, the more likely the behavior will be repeated.
4. The more often reinforcement occurs, the more likely the student will repeat the act.
5. Absence or even delay of reinforcement following an action weakens the probability that the act will be repeated.
6. Intermittent reinforcement of an act increases the length of time a student will persist at a task without further reinforcement.
7. The learning behavior of a student can be developed or *shaped* gradually by *differential* reinforcement—that is, by reinforcing those behaviors which should be repeated and by withholding reinforcement following undesired acts.
8. In addition to making repetition of an act more probable, reinforcement increases a student's activity, quickens his pace, and heightens his interest in learning. These may be called the *motivational effects* of reinforcement.
9. A student's behavior can be developed into a complex pattern by shaping the simple elements of the pattern, and combining them into a chainlike sequence.*

[8] It should be recognized that most laboratory studies involve animals rather than students. These generalizations, then, are still hypotheses rather than "laws."

* For a definition of terms used in reinforcement theory, see the annotated bibliography at the end of this chapter.

short, reinforcement theory provides a rationale for believing that a complex body of learning can be separated into its smallest components. Through it, the student can be taught to master all the subject matter by reinforcing or not reinforcing his responses to successive steps, according to the accuracy or inaccuracy of his replies. The act of not reinforcing an erroneous response is known as *extinguishing.* By discriminating use of reinforcement and extinction the learning program enhances the likelihood that correct responses will be repeated, whereas incorrect responses will be eliminated. Besides shaping the student's behavior, reinforcement also should inspire him to be aware at all times that he *is* learning. Furthermore, it should persuade him to know *what* he is learning. And, finally, it should help him to regard his learning experience as enjoyable and, hence, should motivate him to partake of further learning activity.[9]

Reinforcement Theory and Classroom Practice

The Skinner theory supplied the ingredient missing from Pressey's experiments. It provided the idea of programming instructional materials that Pressey's machines needed. As a student engages in self-instruction, a teaching machine of some sort presents him with an orderly progression of learning matter. The items composing the program pass before him in individual pieces. For each of these he has the opportunity to answer a question, solve a problem, or in some way demonstrate that he has acquired the information. He then promptly compares his reply with the correct response communicated to him by the machine. When he is correct, the machine so informs him and he may advance to the next item, which may be more complex; when he is mistaken, the machine advises him of his error and directs him forthwith to corrective action.

For each item the machine supplies the student with certain

[9] For a fuller, technical description of reinforcement theory, see the annotated bibliography at the end of this chapter.

information, or clues, that aids him to respond accurately. This part of the item is known as the *stimulus.* The remaining portion, which requires the participation of the student, is known as the *response.* To complete a step the student fills in the blank space contained in the item and checks it against the machine's correct answer. Consider a typical item in a program of learning material as illustrated in Figure 1-1.

A chain of steps or a *programmed sequence* for a semester of a single subject might consist of 2500 to 5000 such items—and perhaps more. The items are so planned and interconnected as to increase in difficulty as the student advances to higher degrees of knowledge and greater skill.

The reinforcement theory has the further merit of complementing a body of educational beliefs long utilized in classroom teaching. Ever since the publication in 1898 of *Animal Intelligence* by Edward L. Thorndike, educators generally have accepted a series of findings that have been classified under the broad heading of *stimulus-response theories.* Thorndike and his followers each contributed evidence to show that a learner, impelled by a stimulus, responds in a way calculated to conquer

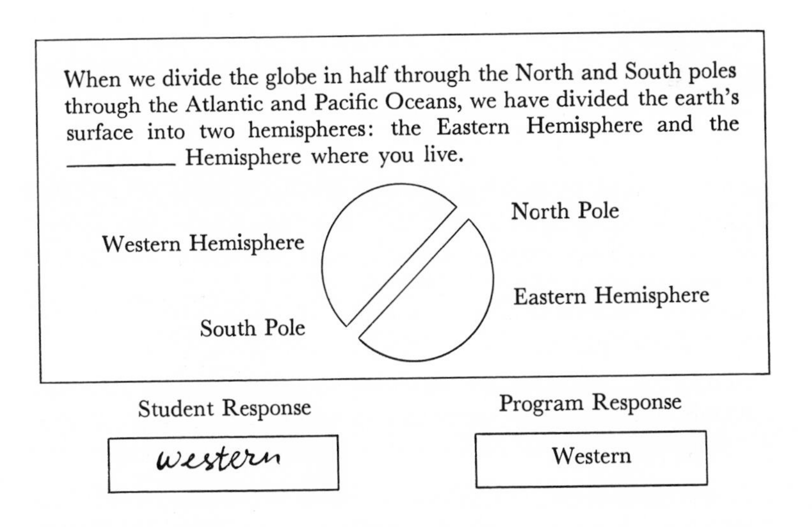

Figure 1-1

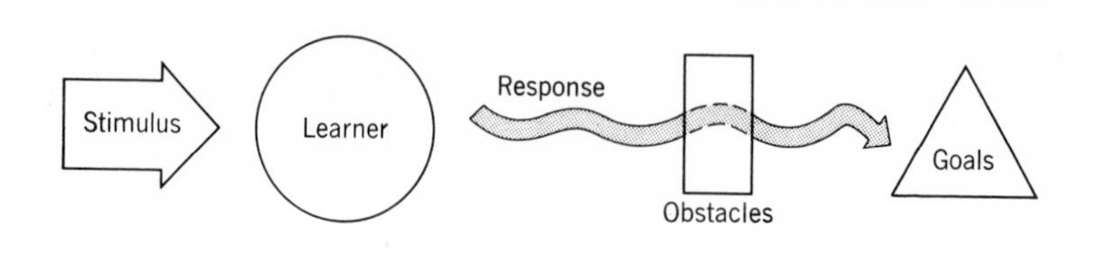

Figure 1-2 A *simplified* illustration of events occurring in stimulus-response learning.

obstacles and carry him to his goal.[10] The stimulus-response procedure figured in the planning of teaching units and in educational experiences long before Holland and Skinner incorporated the principles of reinforcement theory in their first programmed learning course in 1958. One important difference, however, distinguished theoretical views from classroom applications. Whereas the stimulus-response theories, developed to explain the learning behavior of *individual* students, almost always dealt with *groups* of learners in practical applications of lesson planning, reinforcement theory and programmed learning re-emphasized the importance and uniqueness of each student's own learning pattern, and urged that the teacher act, as well as think, in terms of individualized instruction.

Actually, programmed learning may be considered as a return to the fundamentals of teaching to the extent that theories of stimulus-response learning are familiar to classroom teachers. It even might be regarded as the ideal example of the classic stimulus-response model. In any case, programmed learning certainly does not break completely from previous methods of teaching.

By examining a graphic representation of what happens in stimulus-response learning, as shown in Figure 1-2, it becomes possible to form several generalizations about how programmed learning affects the learner, the stimulus, the response, the

[10] Certainly one of the best descriptions of the theories, and connections among the research, of Thorndike, Guthrie, Hull, Watson, and Skinner, is in Ernest R. Hilgard, *Theories of Learning,* second edition, New York: Appleton-Century-Crofts, 1956.

obstacles, the goals, and the total educational process in the classroom.

Some of the things programmed learning does is to make each learner's experience an individual affair and to maintain a constant interaction between a student and its learning material. As it strengthens the motivation to learn by frequent reinforcement, so does it cut down frustration by placing mastery of subject matter within any student's grasp. Moreover, programmed learning improves the student's readiness—or *set*—to learn by keeping him alert and busy.

Programmed learning affects the stimulus by acquainting the student with only one item at a time and by presenting the total number of stimuli in a sequence that leads to greater understanding. It governs the response through instant checks of replies and through consistent, immediate reinforcement of the learning it wishes to impart. Similarly, it closes the door to faulty information by denying reinforcement altogether, and then helps students to rectify their errors through the medium of the program itself.

As to obstacles in the path of progress, programmed learning insists that each single point be understood before the student moves along to the next one, limiting itself at each step to that material for which the student has been prepared. Besides, it offers a mechanism for coping effectively with the range of individual differences in ability among students.

Finally, programmed learning demands the selection of concrete goals before the construction of a program is undertaken. It charts the route to the ultimate goal through a series of intermediate stages and fashions complex subject matter by linkage of discrete, simple items. As a result of these varied influences, programmed learning approximates as closely as possible the acknowledged theoretical model of stimulus-response pedagogy. It affords the best opportunity for individualized tutelage, for constant evaluation of a student's progress, and for unremitting review of the program's own effectiveness in achieving its educational objectives.

If these generalizations about programmed learning are at all valid, corroborating evidence ought to emerge from research into classroom use of programmed material.

Early Studies on Programmed Learning[11]

In 1934, James K. Little, an associate of Pressey who used the unsophisticated programs and rudimentary machines available at the time, concluded that students profited markedly when informed immediately of the accuracy of their response to individual test items. His was the first systematic study of the impact on learning of auto-instructional methods and devices.[12] Although all students tended to gain from the new techniques, the greatest benefits accrued to those in the lower half of the class. Subsequent studies from 1948 to 1950, all leaning on the test approach of Pressey's original work but not yet employing material organized in the sense of later reinforcement theory, substantiated the view that prompt knowledge of results enhanced the capacity of the student to learn.[13–17]

Ten years later came the first experimental results reflecting reinforcement theory. At both second- and sixth-grade levels, Douglas Porter observed that pupils learning spelling with the assistance of programmed material and teaching machines achieved more than pupils taught by the more conventional

[11] It is recognized that many of the studies in this section leave much to be desired in methods and controls. They constitute the majority of reported research, however, and are useful as indicators. Firm conclusions must await further experimentation.

[12] Little, *op. cit.* (Lumsdaine and Glaser, pp. 59–65).

[13] Jensen, B. T., "An Independent Study Laboratory Using Self Scoring Tests," *Journ. Educ. Res.*, 1949, 43, 134–137.

[14] Angell, G. W., "Effect of Immediate Knowledge of Quiz Results on Final Examination Scores in Freshman Chemistry," *Journ. Educ. Res.*, 1949, 42, 391–394.

[15] Angell, G. W., and M. E. Troyer, "A New Self-Scoring Device for Improving Instruction," *School and Society*, 1948, 67 (Lumsdaine and Glaser, pp. 66–68).

[16] Briggs, L. J., "The Development and Appraisal of Special Procedures for Superior Students and an Analysis of the Effects of "Knowledge of Results,'" *Abstracts of Dissertations, 1948–49*, Columbus: Ohio State University, 1950, pp. 41–49.

[17] Pressey, S. L., "Development and Appraisal of Devices Providing Immediate Automatic Scoring of Objective Tests and Concomitant Self-Instruction," *Journ. of Psych.*, 1950, 29 (Lumsdaine and Glaser, pp. 69–88).

method.[18] Holland also reported the success he had with programmed material which he and Skinner employed in courses in behavioral psychology at Harvard University.[19] Even after expanding the number of items in the program from 1400 to 1800, as a consequence of evaluating student responses to the program, errors by students were cut by almost half, and the total time required to complete the subject matter was reduced.[20]

Toward the close of the fifties and the start of the sixties the number of studies increased. Most of them, if not all, have verified the aforementioned generalizations about programmed learning. John Blyth, for example, summarized his experience in teaching logic on a programmed basis at Hamilton College in this way: "We wasted no class time on routine checking or drill. In the classroom we could presuppose a common background of experience. We could usually count on a working command of basic concepts and principles. There was a great increase in interest and improvement in morale." [21] Against this background of student preparation, Blyth reported greater achievement—higher grades, fewer failures, and a decrease in the actual time spent in class by his students.

And so it went. Some research found that programmed materials used in a high school physics course added significantly to achievement when employed as a supplement, and that such materials could be counted on to supply instruction independent of lectures and recitations.[22] Still other experimental results were reported favorably in such diverse places as New York City, Richmond, Indiana, Oberlin, Ohio, Charlottesville, Virginia,

[18] Porter, Douglas, "Some Effects of Year Long Teaching Machine Instruction" (Galanter, pp. 85–90).

[19] Holland, James, "A Teaching Machine Program in Psychology" (Galanter, pp. 69–82).

[20] Holland, James, "Teaching Machines: An Application of Principles from the Laboratory," paper delivered at Educational Testing Service Invitational Conference on Testing Problems, October, 1959 (Lumsdaine and Glaser, pp. 215–228).

[21] Blyth, John W., "Teaching Machines and Human Beings," *The Educ. Rec.*, April, 1960 (Lumsdaine and Glaser, pp. 401–415).

[22] Klaus, David J., "Some Observations and Findings from Auto-Instructional Research," Pittsburgh, Pa.: American Institute for Research, October, 1960, mimeo.

and Los Angeles.[23–27] As these findings became known, they gained adherence even beyond the walls of schools and the borders of campuses.

Other educational systems followed the schools, colleges, and universities into the new fields of programmed learning. Industrial training specialists concerned with educating adults found ways to apply learning programs to their problems. Several leading corporations have begun to try learning programs in their company classrooms, among them Bell Telephone Laboratories, the Polaroid Corporation, Corning Glass Works, and the Hughes Aircraft Company. And International Business Machines and the Eastman Kodak Company already have studied the efficiency of this new industrial training method.[28]

Similarly, public agencies, civilian and military, local, state, and national, have investigated the benefits to be obtained from programmed instructional materials in their own training activities. In 1961, the Air Force said of an experimental installation of teaching machines and learning programs at Keesler Air Force Base, Biloxi, Mississippi, "The automated teaching method in the first test with completely untried materials, taught as well as an experienced live instructor . . . a substantial reduction in training time seems well within our reach."[29] A year earlier the Air Force stated in summarizing its experience on the use of a teaching machine for its SAGE (Semi-Automatic Ground

[23] Komoski, P. K., "Automated Teaching Project, Collegiate School," New York: Center for Programed Instruction, May, 1960.

[24] Barlow, J. A., "Earlham College Student Self-Instructional Project, First Quarterly Report," 1959, mimeo (Lumsdaine and Glaser, pp. 416–421).

[25] Van Atta, Loche, "Research Notes," *Automated Teaching Bull.,* Vol. 1, No. 2, December, 1959, p. 47.

[26] Banghart, F. W., "An Experiment with Teaching Machines and Programmed Textbooks," Charlottesville, Va.: University of Virginia, undated, mimeo.

[27] Roe, Arnold, et al., "Automated Teaching Methods Using Linear Programs," Report No. 60–105, Los Angeles: University of California, Department of Engineering, December, 1960.

[28] Lysaught, J. P. (Ed.), *Programmed Learning: Evolving Principles and Industrial Applications,* Ann Arbor, Mich.: Foundation for Research on Human Behavior, 1961.

[29] Benson, Eugene, and Felix Kopstein, "Machine Teaching of Basic Electronics at Keesler Air Force Base: An Experiment and Results," paper delivered at DAVI Convention, Miami, April 24, 1961, pp. 3–4.

Equipment) system, "The SAGE direction center staff's initial enthusiasm for use of a teaching machine in on-the-job training was sustained over a 16-month period despite the observed implementation problems." [30]

It would seem fair to say that research in the use of auto-instruction has affected every part of the American educational structure. From elementary students to adult trainees, from college classrooms to Air Force installations, experiments have probed the potentialities of programmed learning. But this research is only a beginning. Much more has to come before it becomes possible to assess this new learning method adequately. Nevertheless, even now, despite the insufficiency of experimental data, the developing scene of programmed learning may be examined with interest, and fascinating prospects begin to appear.

Some Generalizations from Research [31]

In the light of the findings thus far, several tentative statements may be made about programmed learning. First of all, it *can* be effective; students have learned successfully from it.[32] Second, programmed learning *can* reduce student error; proper analysis followed by suitable revision of the material can decrease errors even further during the learning process.[33] Third, a learning program tends to level the differences in learning capacities among students; while all students exposed to the program may demonstrate achievement, the gain seems to be more conspicuous among the lower portion of the class distribu-

30 Mayer, S. R., "Use of a Teaching Machine for Air Force On-the-Job Training in the Sage System," AFCCDD-TN-60-51, Washington, D.C.: U.S. Department of Commerce, Office of Technical Services, p. 15.

31 Again, we feel it necessary to state a general *caveat* concerning the studies reported. Many of these pioneering research efforts lacked controls that should be incorporated into future studies.

32 Krumboltz, John D., and Ronald Weisman, "The Effect of Overt vs. Covert Responding to Programed Material," *Journ. Educ. Psych.,* April, 1962.

33 Holland, James, "Teaching Machines: An Application of Principles from the Laboratory," paper delivered at Educational Testing Service Invitational Conference on Testing Problems, October, 1959 (Lumsdaine and Glaser, pp. 225–228).

tion.[34] This might result from both the varying time limit, which permits slower learners to progress at their own rates of speed, and the fact that any programmed sequence tends to impose a ceiling on what anyone can learn. Fourth, individual learning time may vary widely since students work at their own speeds.[35] Fifth, predictability of individual success may decrease because slow learners and others may perform better on programmed material than would have been indicated by previous behavior on other methods of learning.[36] And, sixth, motivation to learn indeed may increase because of students' immediate knowledge of success.[37]

In view of these broad observations, it would seem desirable for teachers, trainers, and administrators to familiarize themselves with the specifics of programmed learning. As a learning method, its sources lie deep in the history of education. Its applications of theory have been described by Dean William Fullagar of the College of Education, University of Rochester, as "those which the best of teachers try to apply in the classroom." Its initial results have been so positive that they command further trials and prolonged examination.

Characteristics of Programmed Learning

A learning program, as has been noted, is a carefully ordered and organized sequence of material to assure the best possible learning conditions for a student. It utilizes the principles of reinforcement to make certain that learning actually does occur.[38] The program embraces both the factual matter of the subject and the skills involved in learning patterns, using every aspect

[34] Lysaught, *op. cit.*, pp. 69–72, and Little, *op. cit.* (Lumsdaine and Glaser, pp. 59–65).

[35] Eigen, Lewis D., "Some Problems in Field Testing Programs for Teaching Machines," *Journ. Educ. Soc.*, Vol. 34, No. 8, p. 375.

[36] Little, *op. cit.* (Lumsdaine and Glaser, p. 65).

[37] Blyth, *op. cit.* (Lumsdaine and Glaser, p. 406).

[38] We wish to acknowledge that our formulation of these points was suggested first by David J. Klaus of the American Institute for Research in comments he made in October, 1960, in "Some Observations and Findings from Auto-Instructional Research," Pittsburgh, Pa.: American Institute for Research, 1960, mimeo.

of reinforcement theory to lead a student to a full understanding of its material. Thus, the program and the person who devises it bear the major responsibility for the student's success. If the student commits errors or fails to master the subject matter, the fault is the program's, not the student's.

Successful programs should embody a number of common characteristics which, taken together, are the identification mark of programmed instructional matter.

1. *Assumptions stated clearly in writing.* A program builder has to make certain assumptions about the student to whom his program is directed. One of these is that he reads at a particular level of competence. Another is that he has a command of vocabulary that is consistent with the language of the program. A third pertains to the student's background in the subject matter. Together, these and whatever other assumptions must be considered for the clear presentation of a specific subject should be put down explicitly in writing before the program maker begins to arrange his learning material.

2. *Explicitly stated objectives.* The program designer must determine the goals—or objectives—of the learning program. These include the defining of those knowledges, skills, and attitudes that the student is expected to acquire through completion of the program. As far as possible, all the objectives should be defined in *operational, observable, measurable* terms in order to facilitate the construction of the program and its subsequent evaluation.

3. *Logical sequence of small steps.* Subject matter, broken down into fragments of information, is arranged in an orderly sequence of growing difficulty so that the student may progress steadily from one point in the program to the next. Not only does this logical, deliberate development of the learning material simplify the acquisition of knowledge, it also tends to reduce the number of student errors because the previous steps have prepared the student to respond correctly to the new stimuli. Small steps emphasize the *gradual* nature of the increase in complexity and the smoothness of the transitions from one item to the next. Moreover, the change is one of quality as well as quantity, for the information grows in both depth and amount at each step.

4. *Active responding.* Programmed learning requires interaction between the student and the program. In the first few items

of any program, for instance, the stimuli usually are so arranged that the responses they seek are quite simple. They may ask a student to fill in a blank, count the number of coins in a row, or complete a series of numbers. As the student complies and receives reinforcement for doing so correctly, he establishes a pattern of stimulus-response interaction. He recognizes that he must respond actively to each stimulus to reach his learning objectives; he cannot progress by remaining passive.

5. *Immediate feedback of information.* As soon as a student makes each response, the program informs him of his correctness or incorrectness. The more rapidly this check—or *feedback*—follows his responses the more effective becomes reinforcement or extinction, as the case may be. This is of vital importance because reinforcement theory stresses that a student learns from the consequences of his responding, not from the making of responses itself. At each step the student is thus informed of how well he is doing. The check keeps him from compounding error.

6. *Individual rate.* For a long time educators have recognized that students learn any single unit of material at different rates. There are, in fact, even differences in the rate at which an individual student learns various kinds of subject matter. These differences in the rate of learning—and all that they imply about needed review, repetition, and additional materials—have been taken into account in the theoretical aspects of learning. Because a learning program generally permits a student to hover over a single item as long as he desires, because it contains, as we shall see later on, built-in items for review, and because the several techniques of programming allow a student to proceed rapidly or slowly according to his own accomplishments, programming can be said fairly to accept and take advantage of individual differences in the rate of learning.

7. *Constant evaluation.* The use of programmed materials enables a teacher to keep two constant gauges on learning activity. The first concerns the program. From examining the student responses to the items he can obtain an approximation of the program's success. Large numbers of errors, particularly large amounts of mistakes on specific individual items or sequences, signify that the designer of the program has taken too much for granted, or has not confined himself to *small* steps, or

has not developed the content with sufficient clarity. The teacher thus gathers objective data upon which to improve the program.

The second gauge is on the student's progress. Not only can the teacher keep track of each student's position in relation to the entire program, but he also can pinpoint his assistance whenever one member of his class runs into difficulty. This more exact knowledge about the progress of every student allows him to plan other learning experiences of a meaningful and helpful kind.

Some Comments on These Characteristics

Although agreement is general on the principles and characteristics of programmed learning, there is certainly no unanimity on how they should be applied in actual programming. For instance, in examining the selection of a paradigm for programming, differing analyses appear as to what constitutes a small step. We find there is agreement that responding by the student should be active, but disagreement on the degree of activity that is essential to assure learning. For example, is selection of a response from a listing of alternatives sufficiently active, or must the student construct his answer without benefit of a multiple-choice grouping? These and similar questions will be treated in the chapter on programming paradigms; it is important here only to point out that there is no one way to utilize these principles and characteristics.

What Programmed Learning Is Not

By this time, the reader should have a fair understanding of what programmed learning is. It is equally important to have a good idea of what programmed learning is *not*. Misconceptions about it abound.

Programmed learning is not an *audio-visual aid*. Because of the wide interest in the teaching machine, programmed instructional materials often have been considered part of the "new technology" in education. The unfortunate implication of such categorization is that too many teachers are likely to consider programmed learning another audio-visual aid, like films, projectors, recording instruments, and slides developed for classroom use. Most audio-visual aids are either response or stimulus devices, whereas programmed learning is an effort to complete the total educational model—stimulus, response, reinforcement. Although there is valid need for both the audio-visual device and the learning program, and the device may be the medium for presenting the program to the student, it is important to differentiate the mechanical instrument from the educational concept that underlies programmed content.

Programmed learning is not a *test*. Initially, a programmed sequence has the appearance of a test, but there the similarity ceases. A program serves as a coach which guides the student to the end of the course. It is a teaching method, not a testing method. Programmed material seeks to supply understanding; testing, on the other hand, measures that understanding. This distinction is essential to the construction of a good program. The simple developing of items, as in a test, does not provide the organized, orderly sequence for self-instruction that is a primary principle of the programming approach. To construct a test and call it a program places all the burden for learning on the student, whereas an effective program assumes the major portion of that responsibility, enabling any normal student to master its content.

Programmed learning is not a *panacea*. Popular accounts of the success of experiments with programmed material often have bordered on the spectacular. This has produced a sharp reaction among those teachers who believe quite correctly that no one educational method is a cure-all. Programmed learning is a method for imparting knowledge and insight. It is not the *only* method. The decision to use it in preference to alternate methods of instruction has to be based on the objectives of the teacher and the background of the students. Yet the results of the research undertaken so far have been so uniformly favorable that programmed learning makes a strong case for its preference. These results, however, do not suggest that a program can supplant the effective teacher, even though it may carry the bulk of instruction in a particular course or may supplement other methods of teaching, or may be used to enrich the experience of the students.

Programmed learning per se is not a solution to the shortage of capable teachers nor an answer to an inadequate school budget. It may offer some relief in the face of these and other educational problems, but it can help only in the same ways as other advances in teaching and administration. Occasionally one hears that teaching machines and programs will replace teachers. This is wrong. What the program does is to supply the student with the basic information of a given subject and free the teacher from the drill-type exercises he must engage in term after term.[39] While the student thus acquires a foundation in a subject to be ready for the far more important consideration of causes, relationships, and applications, the teacher will be released to undertake more creative assignments with students who have been prepared for the challenge. Indeed, since students will progress at their own varied rates, the task of the teacher will become more complex and even more vital.

As a result of programmed learning, it may become necessary to redefine the role of the teacher. No longer need he bear the full load of informing his students. The teacher will be able—perhaps even required—to devote more of his time to worthwhile discussions with his students, to realistic solving of problems with them, and to more adaptations of the material learned to the individual, personal needs of their various life situations. This demand for more creative, imaginative effort should make teaching even more dynamic and satisfying as a profession. It could easily result in great enhancement of the learning process.

Experience Helps

It is essential for those who plan to work with programs to know how to put them together. This is equally true whether they intend to write programs, to select them from those that are available in commercial markets, to use programmed materials as part of a course, or to obtain a broader professional understanding of the learning processes.

[39] We do not mean to imply that programs can supply only the rote kind of information. Some programs are already developed for involved, conceptual learning. We are suggesting that this liberation of the teacher can be one of the first benefits of auto-instructional methods.

To begin with, there is a manifest shortage of available programs of all kinds.[40] Those that have been prepared for spelling, grammar, algebra, foreign languages, and other subjects do not begin to meet the needs of a school curriculum. Moreover, teachers may discover that the objectives of a commercially marketed program do not conform to those he has developed for his own course. Industrial training specialists find even fewer programs available that may be applied to their instructional needs. In many instances, therefore, both teachers and trainers will have to develop their own models in order to measure the utility of the programmed materials available to them in a reasonable manner.

Even if instructors locate commercial programs that seem to cover the subject matter adequately, they should have enough knowledge of the programming process to be able to evaluate the material's applicability to their own requirements. They must note the writer's assumptions, objectives, and techniques, and appraise their value on the basis of existing records of achievement. They must examine the organization of the steps and compare them to their own curriculum. In other words, they must decide on the usefulness and validity of the program. An instructor who has undertaken even a limited amount of programming will be better able to make such decisions, since the experience he has obtained will permit him to make finer discriminations.

Another advantage of experience in this area is its effect on a teacher's professional growth. As one director of instruction in a school system put it, "I am certain that any teacher who does some programming will be a better teacher when he has finished the work." Instructors who have constructed a programmed sequence often regard it as challenging an exercise in teaching as any they have experienced. This reaction comes from the fact that programming obliges a teacher to state his objectives concretely and arrange his materials, item by item, in a way that will assure student achievement of those goals. In an almost unprecedented manner, the teacher has to see this material as the student sees it for the first time. This virtually compels the teacher to recognize that his present methods contain numerous undeclared assumptions and mental

[40] For information on available programs see Part B of the Selected Bibliography in the back of this book.

leaps, which he can negotiate easily because of his familiarity with the subject.

The significance of this realization is so great that the teacher, once having developed a programmed sequence, even though he never may use the product in his classroom, will have gained a vast amount of personal insight into the learning process and this will stand him to good advantage. However, the teacher who actually uses the program he constructs will derive even greater benefit.

A final reason for urging instructors to engage in programming activities is the fact that no teacher likes to use any technique, material, or device in the classroom with which he is not thoroughly familiar or comfortable. There is good reason to believe that the wider use of audio-visual aids, for example, is limited chiefly because teachers and trainers lack familiarity with the operation of the many kinds of projectors, and have had too little chance to explore the materials available to them from diverse sources.

Not every classroom teacher will wish to build programmed sequences covering large segments of his course. On the other hand, until a teacher has done some programming and demonstrated to himself that he can control this new pedagogical method, he would be highly unlikely to use it with his students. If he should use it without previous personal experience, he probably would not do so to best advantage.

The Approach

From working with the development of programs and teaching others how to go about it, the authors have devised a process for organizing programmed instructional materials, which elementary, secondary, and college teachers, and industrial trainers have used effectively in their own construction of sequences for use in their classrooms. The route they follow is traced in great detail and illustrated with examples in the next seven chapters of this book. Pursued in proper sequence, the components of the process should lead any reader to successful creation of a learning program.

The process consists of the following activities undertaken in the order in which they are listed. First, there is the selection of the subject matter to be programmed. This is to be followed by preliminary organization which involves three requirements: the making of assumptions about the learners, the declaration of objectives or goals, and the selection of a programming *paradigm*—or model. Once these have been completed, the program builder turns to his programming activity. He orders, or organizes, the subject matter, constructs the steplike programmed sequences, checks their efficiency by trying them out on learners, and edits or revises them on the basis of his findings. Finally, there comes the post-programming phase and further testing. Criteria are analyzed, student achievement is evaluated, and revisions are made as necessitated.

Dynamics of Program Construction

Figure 1-3 illustrates graphically how the elements of the programming process lead naturally from one to another. The selection of the subject to be programmed requires an assumption by the program builder about the learner who will use the

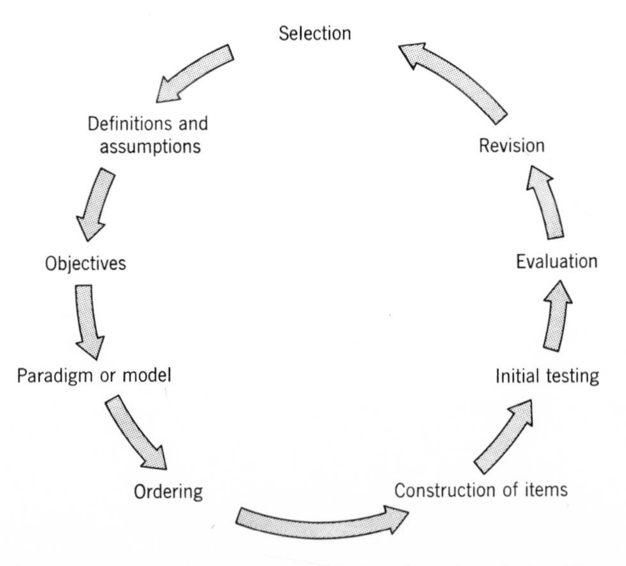

Figure 1-3 *Selection* and succeeding steps in dynamic relationship.

program. Next, he lists the objectives of the materials to be programmed. These factors then influence the programmer's choice of a paradigm for the arrangement of the items.

He can now order the subject matter in the best possible sequence and construct the items in accord with established learning techniques. As soon as short sequences have been completed they can be tested and revised on an initial basis. Later, after exposure to a larger number of students, the sequences can be analyzed for errors and shortcomings. Besides, the sequences can be evaluated for effectiveness in terms of how the student learns from them, and this information can be used for revision of the program. The complete experience has a cyclical quality since it may be used as an aid in the selection of subsequent units of subject matter for programming.

In addition to this one-directional passage through the process, there is a continuous series of checks, which extends throughout the cycle. After the programmer has chosen his unit for programming, he may discover, for example, that his assumptions require him to modify that selection. He may find after considering the abilities of his learners that his choice of subject matter has been too advanced or too elementary. Similarly, his declared objectives should serve as a check on both his selected unit and assumptions. The objectives could show him that he has packed too much into the unit, and that a sifting of material might be desirable. The objectives also might trigger a revision of, or an addition to, his assumptions.

As a consequence of this constant checking, the program builder can make detached decisions about his material at every point in the programming cycle. He can always recognize whether his effort actually is directed along the lines he has elected. Although such relentless re-examination may seem cumbersome, it really simplifies each successive phase in the development of the program, especially when the programmer begins to lay out his sequence of items.

Figure 1-4 illustrates the continuing two-directional development of programmed matter with each step functioning as a springboard for the next one, and as a re-examination of what has happened before it.

We have now explored the origins and fundamentals of programmed learning. Next we shall consider its anatomy. In

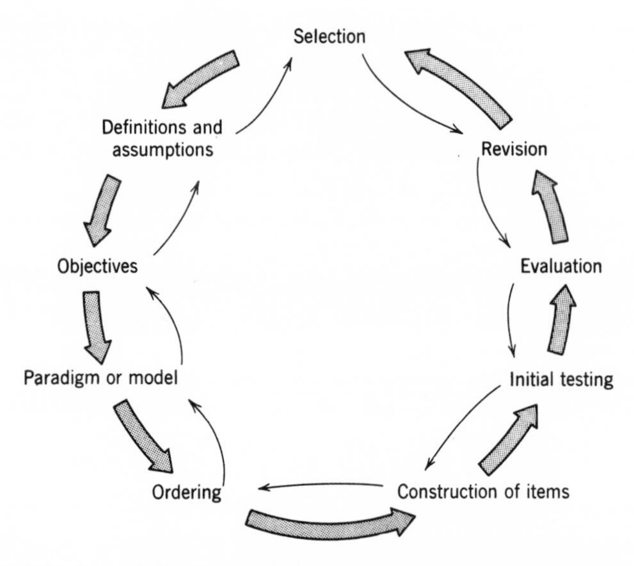

Figure 1-4 Interrelationships between steps in programming process.

the following chapters, composing part two of this book, we shall undertake a microscopic examination of how programs are constructed, inspecting the process phase by phase from start to finish. In the final section of the book, we shall survey the implications and applications of programmed learning. The object of the total exercise will be to show how programmed materials may be introduced into the classroom and to indicate their value in solving the curriculum and special needs of modern-day education.

SELECTED READINGS

1. Cram, David, *Explaining "Teaching Machines" and Programming,* San Francisco: Fearon, 1961.

Here is a short programmed introduction to the principles of programming. It provides both content and example.

2. Galanter, Eugene (Ed.), *Automatic Teaching: The State of the Art,* New York: John Wiley and Sons, 1959.

Gagne, Robert M., and Robert C. Bolles, "A Review of Factors in Learning Efficiency," pp. 13–53.

Galanter, Eugene, "The Ideal Teacher," pp. 1–13.

These introductory articles to the "state of the art" provide a frame of reference for the principles and techniques of programming.

3. Galanter, Eugene (Ed.), *Automatic Teaching: The State of the Art,* New York: John Wiley and Sons, 1959.

Kendler, Howard H., "Teaching Machines and Psychological Theory," pp. 177–185.

Zeaman, David, "Skinner's Theory of Teaching Machines," pp. 167–175.

These articles discuss—and take some exception to—the prevailing theories associated with programmed learning. They should be noted for their contribution to a better understanding of the programmed learning process.

4. Hilgard, Ernest R., *Theories of Learning,* second edition, New York: Appleton-Century-Crofts, 1956.

In addition to the treatment of Skinner's operant conditioning, the reader may choose to look over the discussion of stimulus-response learning from Thorndike's connectionism through Watson, Guthrie, and Hull.

5. Holland, James G., and B. F. Skinner, *The Analysis of Behavior,* New York: McGraw-Hill, 1961.

This selection serves a double purpose. It is an excellent discussion of the theory underlying programmed learning. Additionally, it is the most famous example of programmed material to date. The reader can develop an understanding of reinforcement theory and, at the same time, acquire an appreciation for the construction of a programmed learning map.

6. Keller, Fred S., *Learning Reinforcement Theory,* New York: Random House, 1954.

This is a brief but well-written introduction to reinforcement theory.

7. Lumsdaine, Arthur A., and Robert Glaser (Eds.), *Teaching Machines and Programmed Learning: A Source Book,* Washington, D.C.: NEA, 1960.

Carr, W. J., "A Functional Analysis of Self-Instructional Devices," pp. 540–562.

Lumsdaine, Arthur A., "Teaching Machines: An Introductory Overview," pp. 5–22.

For those interested in a brief, analytic view of the field, these introductory articles will be helpful.

8. Lumsdaine, Arthur A., and Robert Glaser (Eds.), *Teaching Machines and Programmed Learning: A Source Book,* Washington, D.C.: NEA, 1960.

Pressey, S. L., "A Third and Fourth Contribution Toward the Coming 'Industrial Revolution' in Education," pp. 47–51.

Skinner, B. F., "The Science of Learning and the Art of Teaching," pp. 99–113.

Perhaps these two articles might be termed the "classics" in the emerging field of programmed learning. In addition to the two cited, other articles by Pressey and Skinner reproduced in the source book will be of interest to the reader.

9. Margulies, Stuart, and Lewis D. Eigen (Eds.), *Applied Programed Instruction,* New York: John Wiley and Sons, 1962.

Cook, Donald, and Francis Mechner, "Fundamentals of Programed Instruction," pp. 2–14.

Goldberg, Irving A., "An Introduction to Programed Instruction," pp. 15–20.

Short, readable introductions to the principles and techniques of programmed learning.

10. Markle, Susan Meyer, et al., *A Programed Primer on Programming,* New York: Center for Programed Instruction, 1961.

Another programmed introduction to the field combining content with example.

11. Stolurow, Lawrence M., *Teaching by Machine,* Cooperative Research Monograph No. 6, Washington, D.C.: U.S. Department of Health, Education, and Welfare, 1961.

This is a brief and inexpensive paperback. It serves as a general overview of the principles and applications of programmed learning. Some sections may be more detailed than necessary for a beginning programmer, particularly the discussions on machines and their applications.

Chapter Two

Selecting a Unit to Be Programmed

The most natural statement for an individual about to construct a program for the first time is, "I majored in and *know* the field of mathematics. Besides, I *teach* mathematics. I would like to program geometry or trigonometry." After he has had a chance to look over tentative models for programming, has discussed his choice with available instructors and fellow programmers, and has gained some experience in programming sample units, he usually decides that he has bitten off too big a piece to digest at once.

For example, a course in trigonometry generally includes angles, trigonometric functions, special and complementary angles, fundamental identities, right triangles, unit circle and line values, graphs and equations, double and half angles, product formulas, logarithms, logarithmic tables, various solutions of triangle problems, terms, definitions, and many other components. Any one of these could provide a challenging start to the novice. From his own experience, he actually might wish to narrow the project still further.

How far overambitious intentions may have to be curbed is seen from the fate of the student programmer who set out to plan a course on the Constitution of the United States during a two-week workshop. At the end of the session, he found he had managed to complete items covering only the Preamble.

Programming takes time! The rigorous analysis of both the

subject matter and the teaching method simply does not lend itself to swift, broad activity. And to forestall disappointment to beginners, it is best to underscore—perhaps overemphasize—the fact that preparing programs is time consuming. Of course, as an individual gains experience his speed of developing items tends to increase. As he works his way through the programming process, he finds each step an aid, rather than a hurdle, for later sequence construction.

The Role of Criteria

What, then, needs to be done to assure selection of an appropriate unit to be programmed so that what eventually occurs is a worthwhile experience for the new programmer—one in which the pertinent programming factors have been considered? Most important is the establishment of a set of interrelated criteria that provide the programmer with frames of reference for his own endeavors. The selection of the unit to be programmed should be made only after the individual has checked it against these criteria, singly and in concert, in terms of what he seeks to accomplish. Six criteria predominate. They are the programmer's own field of study, the ease of treatment, length, depressed level of learning, logical order of material, and the exclusiveness of special student needs. Let us consider these in depth.

1. *The programmer's own field of study.* The example at the outset of the chapter showed how a novice decided to develop a programmed sequence covering a significant portion of his own field of knowledge only to learn after some floundering that he had undertaken too great a task for an initial effort. Thus, even after considerable experience in his field of study, a programmer cannot rely on this criterion for unit selection by itself; conversely, it seems folly for a programmer to prepare materials outside the field in which he is most competent. Understanding of a subject is necessary and basic to programming it successfully, but this must be supplemented by additional guides to ascertain where to begin.

Actually, what a programmer *may* know of his own field *may* represent only a portion of its total. This might call for a general examination of all the source material in the field of knowledge. What eventually might be programmed, therefore, might represent the thinking and skill of a number of individuals. The assessment of both similar and differing points of view will help to underline the important material, its logical arrangements, and what might serve utilitarian, esthetic, or other purposes. The general examination can be made by studying current curriculum guides and established texts, by reviewing new materials and suggested departures, by discussing the field with other teachers and curriculum coordinators, and by reflecting on the learning behavior and attitudes of the students with whom the programmer has worked previously. It is well, moreover, for a programmer to have taught students the material, and at the level, he intends to develop.

The extent to which the programmer's own field of study plays a part as a criterion in the selection of a unit for programming may be judged from the following comments of students who have learned to program material on their reasons for choosing a particular area of subject matter. "I am very familiar with this material and many of its applications," said one. "This part of arithmetic is an area of strength for me," said another. "This is my own field of specialization," a third remarked. "I feel that I know this field well enough to plan and construct a sequential program," a fourth volunteered. "This unit falls within my own field, although I do not feel myself to be an expert," said a fifth, adding, "I will need assistance from people experienced in physics, chemistry, and radiation biology, as well as from the radiologist."

In short, the programmer requires basic grounding in the field that his unit is to cover. Yet for all his knowledge and experience, it may be prudent for him to refresh his familiarity with the whole field of learning of which the programmed unit will represent but a part.

2. *Ease of treatment.* Ease in the handling of the material is a valuable asset to the programming venture. The more simple and generally accepted the subject matter, the more easily it can be programmed. This accounts, no doubt, for the number of commercial programs available in beginning algebra and the few, if any, in the dynamics of political power.

It pays to make initial selection so simple that the normal

difficulties of adjusting to a new method of instruction are not compounded—or confounded—by the difficulties of the subject matter. In arithmetic, for example, student programmers might write a sequence on the addition and subtraction of one-digit numbers. The task may be simplified further by supplying the students with detailed assumptions and objectives. Even so, the newness of the process and the adjustment to the technique of constructing items that teach presents a challenge to logic and ingenuity.

This does not mean that the programmer has to go back to the subject matter of the primary grades to begin his development of a sequence. Nevertheless, in developing a new skill, he should start with as simple and as fundamental an approach as possible. If the subject matter contains both simple and complex sub-units, it is desirable to choose one of the easiest at first and progress to the more difficult as skill in programming increases.

Some typical selections made by student programmers illustrate how initial choice can combine an interest in subject matter and a desire for relative simplicity. In the general field of language arts, initial unit selections included the principles of syllabification, long vowel sounds, prefixes, telling time, and punctuation of direct quotations. In arithmetic, two of the subjects chosen were Roman numerals, and introduction to carrying in arithmetic. In social studies, selections included the Preamble to the Constitution, latitude and longitude, and definitions of political positions.

For divers individual reasons, the programmers regarded these units as easy starting points for their introductions to the writing and sequencing of learning programs. Their experiences in carrying their projects to a successful conclusion have encouraged them to consider additional, more complicated ventures.

Some of the reasons cited for selecting units on the basis of ease were, "This is an easy area [spelling] to program since it is easily broken into items." "This unit has a simple, logical structure which should program well." "There is general acceptance of the initial rules for syllabification. This should make programming easier." "This is a small unit from a training course for which we have developed a great deal of background material. It should be programmed with ease." Finally, "We have covered this material previously with a set of activity cards. Last year many of the teachers experimented with these cards and found them very useful. It seems possible to model a program after these cards, and develop a program fairly easily."

The criterion of ease of treatment encourages beginners to consider only simple material for their initial units, and to choose one in which the subject matter alone does not present a formidable problem. Later, the programming process itself will assist the teacher or industrial trainer in the handling of more difficult subject matter, but time and experience must be allowed to exercise their influence.

3. *Length.* The criterion of length has at least two aspects: the program length necessary to achieve the objectives desired for the subject matter; and the amount of time the program requires of the student to complete it. Just as the inexperienced programmer selects a relatively simple unit for his first project, so he should concern himself with the length of his initial program. Instead of programming a full course in arithmetic or grammar, he would make greater strides by confining his effort to a short exercise—a unit of the course, or to a lesson or so. This means that the succeeding phases of the programming process—for example, the stating of assumptions, or the declaration of objectives—would be easier to achieve. It also means that the programmer should reach his goal faster and should be ready sooner to test his sequence.

The quicker the programmer sees the first fruits of his work being used by students as a means for learning, the faster he senses accomplishment. Furthermore, the knowledge of student results and an analysis of their success and difficulties helps immeasurably in the construction of later, longer, and more complicated sequences. Most beginners have found it helpful and satisfying to construct short units which they can use, evaluate, and revise—all in a fairly brief period of time.

The programming of units rather than of courses also produces sequences that can be inserted into the existing curriculum. If the school year has already begun, an instructor can select a short unit of material that is to be studied later in the term, and be fairly confident that he can draft it into a programmed sequence by the time the students are ready to begin work on it.

Later, these units can be fashioned into a sub-course or a complete course, over a period of time—perhaps several semesters. In the meantime, both the programmer and his students can benefit from the small portions that have been programmed.

Most teachers seem to agree that programmed sequences should be inserted gradually into the curriculum. This would seem to be particularly true of units that must be field tested and revised. If all students are able to complete the sequence in a few hours or days, the programmer will then have the information he needs to start revision and improvement. If a sequence has not been effective, there has not been so large a commitment in class time that corrective action cannot be taken promptly and easily. As units are improved as a result of student experience with them, more class time may be spent profitably on the programmed sequences.

Examples of units selected by new programmers under the criterion of length are the 30°-60°-90° triangle, an introduction to nouns, the handling of assets on a balance sheet, the definition and addition of matrices, the critical dimensions of photographic film, the reading of a micrometer, and *l'article partitif.* The limited length of such choices rather than the selection of trigonometry, grammar, bookkeeping, matrix algebra, photography, use of a micrometer, or French grammar has greatly simplified the later work of the teacher-programmer in the programming process.

Choices made in consideration of the criterion of length were explained by reasons such as these: "The content of this program is normally covered in about one week of class in Grade Four"; "this unit constitutes a short, independent part of the arithmetic program," and "the length of the material appeals to me because it can be broken down into units and programmed as my schedule permits."

The freshman programmer should think, then, of a short unit in selecting an area for programming. This will simplify the entire programming process, will permit faster preparation of a usable sequence, and will enable more rapid field testing and revision with less initial investment of class time.

4. *Depressed level of learning.* For a number of teachers and trainers, one factor that has strongly affected the choice of units to be programmed has been the depressed level of learning shown by many of their students who had been taught by cur-

rent methods of instruction. In most cases, this involves the apparent inadequacy of conventional approaches to help such students acquire mastery; in a few cases the teachers thought they had encountered problems only because of the inadequacy of existing instructional materials, or even the lack of them.

Certainly a programmer should pay attention in the selection process to those units in his field of knowledge that are notorious stumbling blocks to students. Without ignoring the criteria of *ease* and *length,* he might prepare a sequence designed to meet the specific hard nuts in the curriculum. In one case, as part of a general course in photography, a great deal of student difficulty was traceable to an inability to handle logarithms in making sensitometric calculations. In a short sequence of approximately 100 frames, the programmer was able to teach the two or three logarithmic manipulations that the student had to master to understand the basics of sensitometry. By using the criterion of depressed learning, the programmer was able to select a unit that was particularly helpful to a large number of students—more so, perhaps, than a longer sequence covering a different portion of the curriculum might have been initially.

Another programmer selected a unit introducing student nurses to the care of patients receiving radiation therapy. Not only was there general agreement among the doctors and nurses that this was an area of depressed learning, but it was also recognized as an area covered all too briefly in available texts. Some of the particular points which they desired to impress upon the students simply were not mentioned in textbooks but had been developed out of the experience of caring for patients.[1] Selection of the unit was natural to fill a gap in the educational process.

[1] There is virtually no textual material to use as a guide to handling patients undergoing radiation therapy. Nurses have known that such patients are under physical and emotional stresses, but they have not known for certain how to cope with these problems. Both nurses and patients are largely ignorant about the effects of radiation treatment. Nurses, for instance, sometimes have seemed apprehensive about working with patients receiving radiation therapy. They seemed uncertain about their own safety and well-being. Also, they did not know what signs to look for in patient behavior. Together with the appropriate doctors, therefore, a programmer developed an instructional sequence on the care of patients undergoing radiation treatment and thereby raised the level of learning.

Other subject units selected largely on the basis of the criterion of depressed learning included classification of animals in biology, proper use of the office telephone, computation with approximate data, long division, multiplication, verb tenses, ratio and proportion, use of an airline timetable, transistor theory, and supply-demand relationships.

From random comments of newly trained programmers, one may realize how the criterion of depressed learning influences the selection of a unit for programming. "This material has been difficult for my fourth grade students to grasp. Perhaps this has been due both to the current presentation by the instructor and the kind of drill material that has been made available to them," said one teacher converted to programming. "This portion of biology often appears as a group of odd facts rather than a part of a discipline. Programming may help in organizing and assembling the subject," another asserted. "This has proven to be an area of instruction where vast individual differences have developed in the past. It is hoped that programming will make it possible to equalize the differences by bringing the lower students along," still another said. "This is an area of *poor* student performance after regular instruction," a teacher reported. A fifth made this observation: "The terms and definitions of this mechanical subject tend to mystify many of the students."

Any particular units known to be areas of student difficulty, or units that have relatively little background material developed to aid the student in problems of understanding all await a programmer's interest.

5. *Logical order of material.* Material that is based on inherent and fairly obvious logic may be programmed more easily than material that is less precise in nature. Individuals programming for the first time will face much less difficulty in developing a sequence on the steps in the photographic development process than in constructing a program on artistic composition in photography.

It is often helpful for the teacher or trainer devising his first sequence to select a unit that contains its own inner logic so that the arrangement of items may be simplified. Many industrial trainers, for instance, have chosen some such procedure as the use of an office copying machine, in which the steps are known and the order follows a fixed pattern. Classroom teachers also have found it advantageous to begin their programming activities with a unit similar to the division of whole numbers or the arrangement of the solar system so that they could adhere to the pattern of the subject matter in fashioning the sequence.

By way of warning, one should not select a unit that could raise problems of logical sequencing. It would not be as simple, for example, to develop a program on the powers of the executive branch of the federal government as it would be to begin with a unit on the separation of powers. By choosing the latter area, the programmer could introduce initial concepts and definitions that would make it easier to program the powers and limits of any of the three branches of government. By starting, on the contrary, with a single branch—say, the executive—one almost inevitably runs head on into relationships with the legislative and judicial branches for which no groundwork has been laid.

Among the units programmed on the basis of the internal logic of the subject matter have been the circulatory system, principles of levers, matter, molecules, and atoms, molecular weights, the use of the Verifax machine, understanding the twelve-channel code in punched-card systems, the structure of photographic film, computing a product-moment correlation, and the types of business organization—sole proprietorship, partnership, and corporations.

How the selection of units has been affected by the criterion of logical order of material may be inferred from these representative observations of confirmed programmers. "The information in this section can be readily assembled into a logical order. . . . Almost all of the conventional texts agree on a single, logical order of development in presentation. . . . In looking at my field of interest, it seems reasonable to say that many other units hinge on an understanding of this basic unit. Once this is programmed, I can go in any of several directions."

Programmers should consider whether they can use the logic of the subject matter to advantage, and should do so if possible. They also should be aware of the internal logic of the subject, if only to forestall the selection of a unit that will pose problems in ordering and sequencing the material to be programmed.

6. *Special student needs.* Many programmers have found it

valuable to select initial units whose consequences either have no relationship to the regular course of study or have a specialized relationship because of student needs.

Although it may seem foolish to undertake a program that does *not* relate to the regular course of study, such a unit can produce real benefit. For instance, one new programmer elected to develop a unit on the use of the slide rule. In his school system, there was no provision in the curriculum for instruction on the slide rule. Yet most of the mathematics and physics teachers agreed that such instruction would be worthwhile, because each year a number of students requested private assistance in learning to handle the instrument. The program proved useful to students in a wide range of grade levels, subject-matter interests, and personal abilities. As such, it became a valuable addition to the school curriculum, helpful to students in many courses, although not directly related to any specific course of study. It still does not appear, for instance, in any of the course syllabi in the school. A similar program on the use of a micrometer has proved to be of equal merit.

Other units have been selected because of their specialized relationship to the course of study. Some of these have been prepared exclusively for use as enrichment material for students who complete the regular materials early; others have been designed specifically for remedial purposes to assist students encountering unusual difficulty in a course. A fifth grade teacher, for example, programmed a unit on entomology, which was designed only for enrichment within the context of the elementary science course. A junior high school teacher programmed a remedial unit on synonyms, antonyms, and homonyms to help a small number of students who displayed extreme weakness in understanding them. Should this sequence seem as though it would fit better under the criterion of depressed learning, for these *few* students the *specialized nature* of the objective was the basis for the selection.

Another asset of this criterion is that it reassures the teacher who may be reluctant to experiment with students in regular course assignments. Often new programmers have been concerned lest their experimental program fail and their pupils not receive adequate instruction in a vital section of the particular subject matter. If a programmer feels this way, he should have no difficulty in finding a topic like the use of the slide rule, for which there may be no current instruction, or a unit like entomology, which can be introduced for the sake of enriching pupils who have mastered the normal course content.

Industrial trainers find this criterion especially helpful. Many of their requests for assistance fall outside the regular courses of instruction carried on within the company. Consequently, they may be more willing to experiment in these areas that are not as closely related to specific training programs.

Other units stemming from this criterion for selection include sharing and teamwork in the classroom, traffic safety, soil erosion and its effects, role playing in communication, the climate of the great plains, bond investment, basic offensive cutting movements in basketball, the teen-ager and the use of alcohol, the automobile fuel system, and a guidance program on "Your Future Employment."

In acknowledging the value of this final criterion of special student needs, the following explanations have been made by newly turned programmers. "This unit is relatively self-contained. Nothing is needed by way of preparation. . . . This is a program in library skills—selected because the librarian has no time to teach. . . . Programming this unit would allow students to work on their own for enrichment while the teacher works with other students. . . . This unit is designed specifically for corrective and remedial reading. My background has highlighted this area of children's needs. . . . This enrichment program is designed to foster attitudes about the subject matter among the faster students."

Some consideration, therefore, has to be given to the exclusive behavioral consequences of a unit selected for programming. It may be chosen either because it lies outside the regular course of study, or because it has a specific, special relationship to the regular course of study, such as review, remediation, or enrichment.

Selecting Programs for Industrial Use

In general, these six criteria for selection all apply to the choice of first programming efforts at all levels of schooling, and for both broad and special uses. Primary and secondary teachers, college professors, and industrial trainers alike should heed, for example, the criteria of field of knowledge and ease. Because of the unique problems of industrial training, however, those engaged in this pursuit have to consider an additional group of guidelines in selecting units for initial programming. They must regard the number of students to be trained, for unlike most school situations, industrial training often has a limited number of trainees in any single subject. While programmed learning may have, in such circumstances, a particular value, the programmer should consider the number of people to be served. The cost of developing programmed material might not be justified if only a few persons are to be exposed to it.

Industrial trainers also must evaluate the permanence of the subject matter. Certain portions of industrial subject matter have a rapid rate of obsolescence. The trainer should consider this before starting to program, and concentrate on those units likely to be useful in the years ahead.

Finally, there is the estimated time for development. The cost of time spent in course development often is criticized in industrial training—and perhaps unwisely so. But the industrial trainer must weigh the time spent in programming particularly in terms of assigning priorities in development. He should seek the highest return for the least investment.

Each of these considerations has to be viewed in the light of the trainer's own company environment and its attitude toward experimentation. Various industrial training specialists have reflected this in their choice of units for initial development. Some sequences were expressly job oriented, some were more in the form of enrichment, whereas others provided review or remedial work for trainees who previously had completed a course of instruction by conventional methods. Among the units chosen by the programmers were such diverse topics as the grained zinc offset lithographic surface plate, a theory of the nature of light, a review of standard practices for supervisors, and the use of a budget.

To conclude, the programmer's first effort ideally should be simple, short, and reasonably ordered. This will lighten his task for each remaining step in the programming process.

SELECTED READINGS

1. Finn, James D., and Donald G. Perrin, *Teaching Machines and Programmed Learning, 1962: A Survey of the Industry,* Occasional Paper No. 3, Washington, D.C.: NEA, 1962.
2. *Programs '62—A Guide to Programed Instructional Materials Available to Educators by September 1962,* The Center for Programed Instruction, New York, in cooperation with the U.S. Department of Health, Education, and Welfare, Washington, D.C., 1962.
3. Rigney, Joseph W., and Edward B. Fry, "Current Teaching-Machine Programs and Programming Techniques," *Aud.-Vis. Comm. Rev.,* Vol. 9, No. 3, May–June, 1961, Supplement 3.

These three references include listings and/or samples from currently available programs. They are of interest to the beginning programmer because they demonstrate the range of topics that have been selected for programming.

4. Smith, B. Othanel, William O. Stanley, and Harlan J. Shores, *Fundamentals of Curriculum Development,* New York: World Book, 1957.

See particularly Chapter VI, "Principles of Subject-Matter Selection," and Chapter VII, "Procedures of Content Selection." Included in the general discussion are five standards for subject-matter selection which should aid the beginning programmer.

5. Tyler, Ralph, *Basic Principles of Curriculum and Instruction* (Syllabus for Education 360), Chicago: The University of Chicago Press, 1950.

The "General Principles in Selecting Learning Experiences," contained in pages 42–44, stress an eclectic approach to selection which will be of help to teachers and programmers.

Chapter Three

Assumptions about Learners

"What I know about writing auto-instructional lessons," John Barlow has confessed, has been "taught me [by] my students." In reply to the self-posed question of who controls whom, he left no doubt that, in the realm of programming, students for whom a program is intended ultimately govern the character of the material and its presentation. For this reason, it is extremely important that teachers and training specialists who expect to make excursions into programming find out as much as possible about the traits of those who will use their handiwork. It is no less important to make basic assumptions from this knowledge about the whole universe of learners for whom any set of educational materials is programmed.

Once a programmer has gathered this information and completed his assumptions, he will make it easier for others to use his program if he includes these facts with it. In a practical sense, this data provides other teachers, professors, and training specialists with more substance than a program title on which to base a decision of whether and how to employ the program. The program should contain in addition an explanation of how the learners contributed to its completion. It should disclose whether they were instrumental in editing the material, accumulating performance data, establishing ranges of diverse accomplishments, comparing the programmed method of instruction with some more conventional one, or some other phase of programming activity.

Essentially, this chapter pursues these matters by focusing attention on three characteristics of learners—their ability, their background, and their purpose. In each instance more than a single source of information may be needed to round out the picture. Accumulated records which most schools keep up to date offer some details. Diagnostic tests also may prove useful. And there are always the personal experiences of the programmer as a teacher or learner himself. All these add up to the sum of how students learn, and the assumptions that have to be made, in writing, about their learning habits.

Ability

The ability of a student may be viewed in several ways, and the differing abilities among a group of students may be summarized diversely.* Ability may be judged from scores obtained on IQ and aptitude tests, on achievement tests, and on reading level tests. Or it may be detected from teacher ratings, such as marks or collection of anecdotal records, from specially devised rating instruments, or from estimates of ability furnished by any other source. For example, the number and kinds of errors committed on a prior programmed unit might reflect the learners' abilities and aptitudes for the subject, as well as shed light on the suitability of the particular program itself.

INTELLIGENCE. A look at intelligence test scores for groups of students can be quite revealing about the learning propensities of the students, since these scores represent past performances. From them, a programmer might infer that one group of learners would take a longer time than a second group, as a rule, to complete the program he has in mind. Or he might conclude that several members of the first group could traverse his program in shorter time than anyone in the second group. Further, he might suspect a higher average rate of error among one group than the other. Finally, he might expect some members of the second group to commit more errors and take more time than any member of the first group.

* For an understanding of the simple, descriptive statistics involved in the preparation of programmed material, see the selected readings.

In so doing, of course, the programmer makes guesses, or states *assumptions,* about the learning prospects of students. But he bases his assumptions on what is known of these students from data on their intelligence. It is important for him early in his undertaking to reach these assumptions predicated, as they are, on statistical information. But even more important, perhaps, may be his willingness to put a program before the students on an experimental or tentative basis, reserving ultimate judgment of the program's effectiveness until he has observed student reaction to it.

Data actually perform a dual role. Not only do they help the programmer to develop his sequence, but they also assist others in reaching decisions as to whether a particular program might fit their own instructional needs. For the new programmer, knowing as much as he can about the intelligence of his students is as valuable a guide to preparing a program as test information obtained from learners on the difficulty of individual items and sequences.

ACHIEVEMENT. Like intelligence, achievement also supplies clues to ability. A group of learners which achieves more or less uniformly and whose members score similarly on achievement tests is likely to evince uniformity in its pursuit of a program. Nevertheless, other factors have to be weighed for the data on achievement to possess validity. An achievement test, at best, only samples performance—or *potential* performance. It does not predict the total expectation. Thus time becomes a subsidiary element to be considered, not in the taking of the test, where it tends to be controlled, but in the acquiring of the knowledge and skills that constitute the achievement demonstrated on the test. If a great range exists in the time that individual learners have devoted to the acquisition, the programmer would have to expect some range of performance on his program. Perhaps the best use of achievement test data in making assumptions about the learner occurs when the exercise includes more than a single subject-area test result, at least one of which is in the same field as the programmer's and contains as complete a statistical description as possible. The other results could be used to examine the variability of performance in related achievement areas, such as critical thinking or problem solving.

READING LEVEL. For younger learners especially, for whom a programmer might be preparing materials, reading level scores assist in the selection of a program's word standard. In his initial sequence, a programmer may find that he has under- or overestimated the reading level of the group for which he is programming. From the success, or difficulty, of the program as it relates to the reading level scores he should be able to stipulate the reading ability desired for successful pursuit of the program. The relatively simple administration of reading tests, especially in the public schools, facilitates a check on reading ability, as scores are available in most institutions. It is clear that the beginner should endeavor to ascertain the reading levels of his students before he sets out to program his material. Data on the reading levels of these pupils, and their relation to other variables such as achievement and intelligence, moreover, would guide other instructors who might be considering the program for their students. Another teacher, by examining the data, has a basis for looking at his own group of boys and girls and deciding whether a program built to such specifications will be suitable for them. The more information he has about the learners for whom the program was designed, the more reasonable his own decision on adoption is likely to be.

DIAGNOSTIC TESTS. In addition to intelligence, achievement, and reading level scores, there are other kinds of data the inexperienced programmer and the user of a program should find informative. High on the list are the results of specially devised diagnostic tests that divulge particular skills and knowledges among learners. For a program on "Ratios in Trigonometry" the diagnostic test in Figure 3-1 was built to demonstrate that every trial learner could complete the program successfully and to assure that all experiences required by the learners were included. Data obtained from administration of the test to the primary learner group yielded the information the programmer needed to make appropriate adjustments to the program.

TEACHER RATINGS. A teacher's ratings of student performance usually are found in the form of traditional letter grades or marks, or of some score based upon a rather informal scaling system of zero to 100, or in anecdotal records. The informative

Diagnostic Test

1. Round off the following to the nearest tenth:
   (a) 35.76 (b) 132.34 (c) 367.55
2. Round off the following to the nearest whole number:
   (a) 1043.769 (b) 982.456 (c) 34.09
3. Solve each of the following equations:

   (a) $3x - 6 = x - 10$

   (b) $\frac{x}{2} - \frac{x}{3} = 2$

   (c) $\frac{2}{b} + \frac{4}{b} - 3 = 0$

   (d) $\frac{5}{x + 4} = \frac{4}{x - 4}$

   (e) $\frac{4}{x} - \frac{2}{x} = \frac{2}{3} - \frac{3}{x}$

4. Complete the statements below:
   (a) Two triangles are ________ if two angles of one are equal to two angles of another triangle.
   (b) A ____________ is a comparison of two quantities by division.
   (c) Corresponding sides of similar triangles are ____________.
   (d) A ____________ is an equation stating that two ratios are equal.
5. Solve for x in each of the following:

   (a) $\frac{x}{5} = \frac{3}{10}$ (c) $\frac{x}{5} = \frac{125}{4}$

   (b) $\frac{5}{6} = \frac{x}{3}$ (d) $\frac{8}{x} = \frac{3}{7}$

6. The two triangles below are similar. Find the lengths of sides a and b in triangle II.

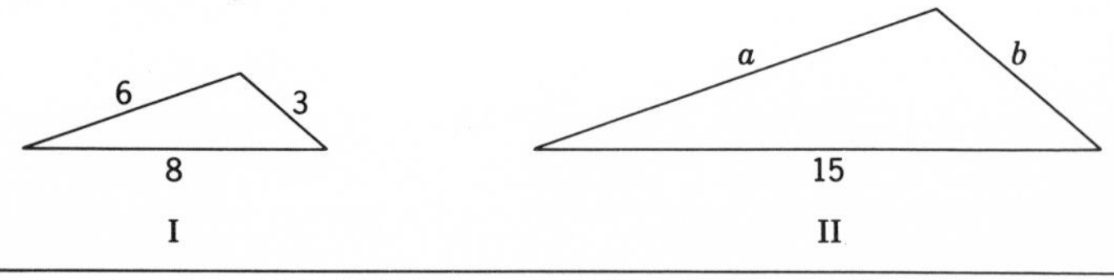

Figure 3-1

aspect of these kinds of data is found by examining a student's record over a period of time or from a number of different teacher estimates. One should look for consistency or wide variation, either among teachers or in time, and compare the findings with any objective data for another consistency check. If a teacher demonstrates that his estimates of student ability as reflected by performance rarely differ from the facts obtained in an objective fashion, then one kind of judgment may be made. If, on the other hand, there is considerable discrepancy between the teacher's estimates of an individual and, for instance, his IQ score, then another type of judgment is indicated.

For example, are we looking at an under- or overachiever? If so, what does this signify for the programmer? If overachievement has been attained because of the student's acceptance of the teacher's standards, will the use of a program in which no grade will materialize cause the student to react differently than he would to some task assigned by the teacher? Answers to questions of this type await willing programmers and teachers—those who wish to discover not only how, but *why,* boys and girls learn. For the present, it is necessary to accept the variables and other problems in human learning while creating a climate of cooperation in educational research. As ways are sought to acquire knowledge of these problems and conditions, the programmer has to increase his understanding of learners by use of the kinds of data discussed.

Background

Background information generally is assumed to include age and grade levels. However, intelligence and achievement data also contain these factors. Consider, therefore, another kind of background data and a somewhat different method of data collection. The two types most common relate to *socio-economic* level and to *urban-rural* considerations. Research [1] accents the importance of understanding socio-economic conditions and

[1] For example, see Lindgren, Henry Clay, *Educational Psychology in the Classroom,* New York: John Wiley and Sons, 1956. Also see Stroud, James B., *Psychology in Education,* New York: Longmans, Green, 1956.

their relation to motivation, personality, and success in school. Yet this is not readily susceptible to assessment by objective means. Most classroom teachers and industrial trainers have neither the time nor the qualifications to conduct detailed studies of socio-economic conditions. Nevertheless, the programmer can contribute to better understanding of these factors by supplying as full a description as possible of the students who use his program during the developmental phase.

The programmer should know the kind of community whence his learners come, the general economic and educational levels of their parents, and the adjustment they have made to the school environment. In these respects, the industrial training specialist has available perhaps even more complete information than the teacher. Job classification, organizational level, and salary brackets are factors that might condition his report on program development.

The authors believe that the programmer has to attempt to describe the background of his trial learner group as carefully and extensively as possible. His efforts will illuminate those examining his program and will prove particularly helpful to other individuals who wish to interpret the program's results.

Purpose

Certainly, a programmer is better able to prepare materials for students if he knows what impels them to learn. In preparing a program for boys and girls who intend to go to college, for instance, he knows from data on intelligence, achievement, and background along with the ultimate objective of the students that they can cope with a higher level of difficulty, and tolerate a greater length than others, and perhaps endure the seriousness that he chooses to incorporate in his writing. If he believes that most of his learners do not plan to go to college but instead intend to work in industry, he can mold his program to match more closely the knowledge and skills they will need. In dealing with students who have technical school as their goal, he can program those kinds of preparatory materials that he knows will be of most use in the future.

Not to be overlooked is the possibility that the climate of the school or industry in which the programmer finds himself might not encourage experimentation. Under these circumstances, he dare not do anything radically different. Instead, he might attempt very short sequences without labeling them "automated teaching," "teaching machine method," or "automatic instruction." He can try these on individuals who can profit from the experience; after he has demonstrated success with the method he could become more ambitious and extend it to the whole group of learners.

In industry, many of the types of data discussed are not available. However, the industrial programmer should make every effort to obtain as many facts as possible about his learners. Now that he is directly involved in the educational process, he may find himself obliged to collect additional information about the learners in order to be enlightened by the kinds of data that guide the teacher.

As most veteran programmers will agree, if so relatively young a field can already have its veterans, almost any effort to uncover the traits of the individuals composing a learner group engages the novice in a profitable exercise. Generally, delving into abilities, aptitudes, achievements, backgrounds, and purposes is a multi-stage undertaking, but it may be pursued in a series of activities. To begin with, a programmer is required to make some assumptions about his learners in order to write something designed to assure that learning will occur. If the programmer doubts the validity of his assumptions, he must commence to gather data about the learners that will impart information about their characteristics. From the several kinds and sources of data, he may gain the insight he needs to make pertinent assumptions upon which to base his program. He can now look back at his criteria for selection of the unit to be programmed [2] and test his original choice in the light of his assumptions.

In checking the criteria against the assumptions about the learners, the programmer should ask himself the following questions:

[2] For review of the criteria for selection of a programmed unit, see the previous chapter.

Must the criteria be changed because of some hitherto unknown characteristic of the learners?

Does the ability of the learners necessitate an increase or decrease in the level of difficulty of the programmed unit?

Is it necessary to include introductory or preparatory materials because of the wide range of past achievement among the learner group?

Are the criteria for unit selection the appropriate ones in view of the abilities and backgrounds of the members of the group?

Will the program satisfy the students' needs to achieve, and meet their purposes?

Does the program affect further instructional patterns?

These and many other questions need to be raised with respect to the dynamics of program planning and preparation. Once a beginner has gone through the process first of selecting a unit to be programmed and then of making assumptions about the learner group for which the unit is intended, it becomes obvious to him that several contingent decisions bear on the nature of the program finally produced. In moving along to successive stages in the programming process, further possibilities for contingent decisions will assert themselves. The next of these turn up in the following chapter which addresses itself to the choosing of reasonable and adequate objectives for a programmed sequence.

SELECTED READINGS

1. Bartz, Albert E., *Elementary Statistical Methods for Educational Measurement,* Minneapolis: Burgess, 1958.

Chapters 1 and 2 discuss simple descriptive statistics useful to the programmer. A good source for the beginner in statistics.

2. Guest, Lester, *Beginning Statistics,* New York: Crowell, 1958.

3. Lindgren, Henry Clay, *Educational Psychology in the Classroom,* second edition, New York: John Wiley and Sons, 1962.

Chapter 4 discusses background relations with family and environment and their effects on personality and behavior.

4. Prescott, Daniel A., *The Child in the Education Process,* New York: McGraw-Hill, 1957.

Part Two is devoted to the understanding of children. All teachers, especially those in elementary schools, should be aware of this material

5. Pressey, Sidney L., Francis P. Robinson, and John E. Horrocks, *Psychology in Education,* New York: Harper, 1959.

"The Nature and Nurture of Abilities," in Chapter 3, should be interesting and useful to a programmer or teacher.

6. Stroud, James B., *Psychology in Education,* New York: Longmans, Green, 1956.

In Chapter 2 relationship is drawn between education and social class. On page 33 begins a discussion on class differences in motivation.

Chapter

Four

Appropriate Objectives

Any teacher who regards his profession as a matter of trust constantly strives to improve his performance. He does so by altering his methods of teaching from course to course or class to class and begins by setting forth his objectives, which may change in the wake of new knowledge and experience. He then selects appropriate content and learning procedures to lead him to the goals he has chosen. By organizing the materials so as to assure efficient progress toward the objectives, he is soon in a position to measure and evaluate results in order to discern how well he is faring.[1]

This practice of the conscientious teacher illustrates the next challenge that the individual who wishes to turn his hand to the programming of self-instructional materials must face. Assuming that he has enough competence in a subject area to select a unit for programming, and that he knows the capacities of the learners for whom the program is intended, the programmer is ready to concentrate on objectives. This is not to imply that only a working teacher can create a sound, functional program. To the contrary, it is the rare individual who can combine extensive program construction with a full-time career in the classroom. The essential point is that after a unit has

[1] Tyler, Ralph W., "The Functions of Measurement in Improving Instruction," in *Educational Measurement,* by E. F. Lindquist (Ed.), Washington, D.C.: American Council on Education, 1951.

been chosen and assumptions have been made about those to whom it will apply, the programmer must then develop in a rather formal manner the goals to be achieved by his program.

Two kinds of objectives concern the programmer. *Immediate* objectives are one of these, and they usually are stated as something concrete to be learned, or as some specific knowledge, understanding, or skill to be acquired. *Ultimate* objectives, the other kind, relate more to the long-range development of the learner and the systematic use of the subject matter.[2] In his endeavors, the programmer should attempt to encompass both types of goals. He should weigh his program, therefore, from two distinctive points of view. On the one hand, the program inculcates immediately useful information that enables a student to solve problems posed by the school and the community environments, or helps him to comprehend the nature of the world around him, or gives him a feeling of accomplishment, which prompts him to learn more. On the other hand, the program fits into a continuum of learning experiences and assists the student to understand the next stages in the sequence, or it adds to the storehouse of knowledge and skills he will need throughout his life and career to cope with the problems that will confront him.

Operational Definitions

In a delightful book, *A Hole Is To Dig*,[3] Ruth Krauss has observed that the word "hole" refers to the result of digging operations by the newly verbal child. She thus illustrates the ways in which children tend to define new words in terms of the experiences and actions that accompany their occurrences. What children do is to define abstractions—that is, words and ideas—on the basis of tangible operations. This is a fruitful lesson for the teacher.

Most of the goals, aims, or objectives that teachers proclaim as desirable are abstract. To the extent that they are abstract,

[2] Noll, Victor H., *Introduction to Educational Measurement,* Boston: Houghton Mifflin, 1957, p. 92.

[3] Krauss, Ruth, *A Hole Is To Dig,* New York: Harper, 1952.

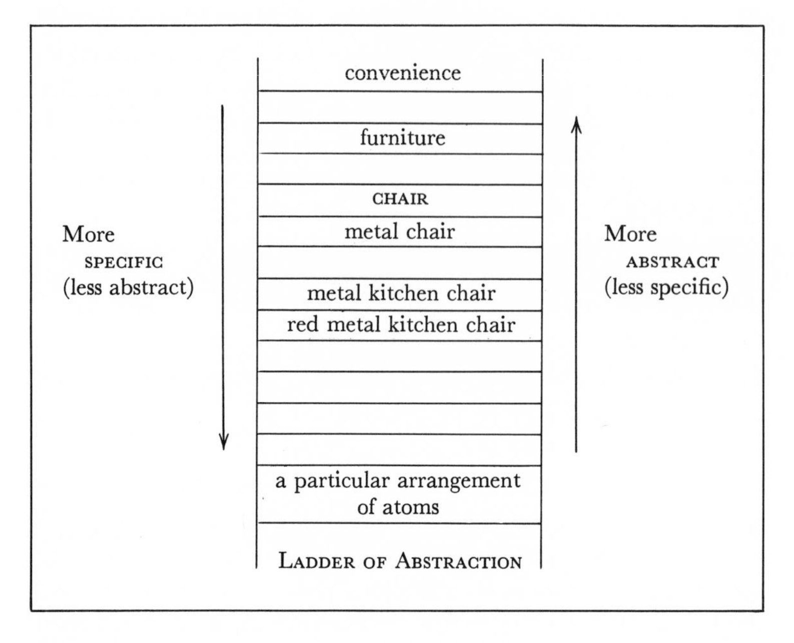

Figure 4-1

they remain vague and are difficult to attain. As teachers become able to discuss their objectives in the light of the operations that define them or, as most educators call them, the *behavioral outcomes of instruction,* they become better instructors and receive much more satisfaction from their work. In so doing, they become *more* operational and *less* abstract about their goals through a struggle to use more specific terminology to elucidate them. For the programmer, the gain in proficiency and gratification is apt to be even greater than for the ordinary teacher. Let us explore the implications of this.

One device that illustrates the process of operationally defining an abstraction is the *ladder of abstraction* seen in Figure 4-1.[4] After noting that it is possible to move either up or down

[4] The Ladder of Abstraction as explained by S. I. Hayakawa in *Language in Thought and Action* (New York: Harcourt, Brace, 1949) comes from "The Structural Differential" as originated by A. Korzybski in his *Science and Sanity: An Introduction to Non-Aristotelian Systems and General Semantics,* Lancaster, Pa.: Science Press, 1933.

the ladder with an abstract concept such as CHAIR, teachers and programmers have been able to transfer the process to their own objectives. That is to say, it is just as possible to increase or decrease the level of abstraction with a device like *chair* as it is with educational objectives. Furthermore, the open rungs in the diagram indicate possibilities for additional ways to make an idea either more or less abstract.

One reason why the transference works, and on which there is wide agreement among teachers and programmers, is that an awareness has been established of a difference—or gap—between the abstract goal and the specific operation. Associated with this is a recognition that steps lie between the polar, semantic positions. After some experience in traversing these steps, using common objects at first and then some common educational objectives, such as "understanding" and "skill" in a particular subject, it becomes relatively easy to develop an acceptance of a *dimension of observability;* that is, as one progresses from the abstract goal to specific operations, the chances increase for observing student behavior. From this development emerges a *dimension of agreement;* that is, as the abstract goal is converted into a concrete operation and as behavior becomes more susceptible to being observed, the observers begin to agree more often about what they have seen. Figure 4-2 illustrates one entire process.

Because many questions arise in the minds of new programmers about the apparent limits of the ladder of abstraction, Figure 4-3 serves to demonstrate that it is possible to move down the ladder in a number of diverse ways. The diagram shows several alternatives for the operational definition of any abstraction and the fact that the choice of any behavioral goal may be questioned. If the objective, "to understand the value of self-discipline," for example, can be defined operationally as one set of goals beneficial to the individual and, contrarily, as a second set *not* beneficial to the individual, then it is clear that the former set should be pursued and the latter ignored. Thus, a basis exists in experience for arranging operationally defined objectives in such a way that tentative priorities can be established for the teacher and the programmer. This is of considerable value to the programmer because it directs his programmed unit toward the most desirable results.

ABSTRACT ↕ OPERATIONAL

Abstraction Ladder	Progression of a Goal from Abstract to Specific	Observability and Agreement Dimension
(Abstract) GOAL:	(for learners) To acquire a basic understanding of earth-sun relationships.	possibly observable, perhaps, to another with same understanding.
(Less abstract) sub-GOAL:	To use the terminology of earth-sun relationships in sentences and paragraphs.	observable by the teacher but without provision for assessment of understanding.
(More specific) sub-GOAL:	To discuss with others the relationships between the sun and the earth, using correct terminology.	observable with some assessment of understanding possible.
(Even more specific) sub-GOAL:	To use the terms *orbit*, *axis*, and *elliptical* in meaningful ways in a paragraph.	observable; can be compared with other performances.
(Very specific) sub-GOAL:	To differentiate correctly between such terms as "revolution" and "rotation" in earth-sun relationships.	directly observable and comparable; "authorities" would generally agree.

Figure 4-2

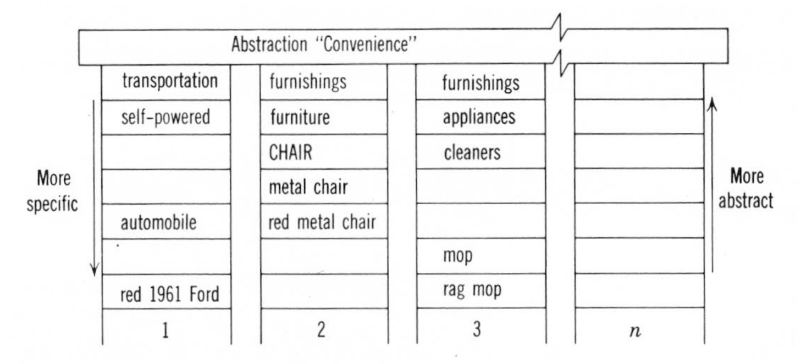

Figure 4-3

This process of questioning and defining operationally *all* the aims of a course of instruction is a much needed experience for programmers. If it can be done, and if cognizance can be taken as a program is developed of what has been accepted and rejected in a culture's educational system, the best ends of that system will certainly be served.

A similar approach to the problem of setting appropriate objectives in terms of behavioral aims has been published recently. This work is unique because the author has used programming as the medium through which to present his material. He has summarized his thesis in this manner: [5]

> A statement of instructional objectives is a collection of words or symbols describing one or more of your educational *intents.*
>
> An objective will communicate your intent to the degree you have described what the learner will be DOING when demonstrating his achievement and how you will know when he is doing it.
>
> To describe terminal behavior (what the learner will be DOING):
>
> (a) Identify and name the over-all behavior act.
> (b) Define the important conditions under which the behavior is to occur (given and/or restrictions and limitations).
> (c) Define the criterion of acceptable performance.
>
> Write a separate statement for each objective; the more statements you have, the better chance you have of making clear your intent.

[5] Mager, Robert F., *Preparing Objectives for Programmed Instruction,* San Francisco: Fearon, 1962.

Although the injunction to establish objectives in a completely operational fashion is a worthy one, the provision of "operational definitions" to prospective programmers invariably raises many questions which, in part at least, should be considered as materials are prepared for use by learners in our society.

The Classification of Educational Goals

A volume of general educational objectives in the cognitive domain[6] has been found to be an extremely useful source book for the new programmer as well as for the more experienced educator who has turned to programming materials. This carefully collected, ordered set of objectives is divided into six discussion areas, each of which is detailed extensively. These areas are knowledge, comprehension, application, analysis, synthesis, and evaluation. The completeness of the resource may be seen from the way in which the area *knowledge* is developed:

1.00 *Knowledge*

1.10 *Knowledge of specifics*

The recall of specific and isolable bits of information—refers primarily to what might be called the hard core of facts or information in each field of knowledge.

1.11 *Knowledge of terminology*

Knowledge of the referents for specific verbal and non-verbal symbols . . . may include knowledge of the most generally accepted symbol referent, knowledge of the variety of symbols which may be used for a single referent, or knowledge of the referent most appropriate to a given use of a symbol.

1.12 *Knowledge of specific facts*

Knowledge of dates, events, persons, places, sources of information, etc.

1.20 *Knowledge of ways and means of dealing with specifics*

Knowledge of the ways of organizing, studying, judging, and criticizing ideas and phenomena . . . includes methods of inquiry, the chronological sequences, and the standards of judgment within a field as well as the patterns of organization through which the areas of the fields themselves are determined and internally organized.

[6] Bloom, Benjamin S., et al., *Taxonomy of Educational Objectives—The Classification of Educational Goals Handbook I: The Cognitive Domain,* New York: Longmans, Green, 1956.

1.21 *Knowledge of conventions*
Knowledge of characteristic ways of treating and presenting ideas and phenomena . . . usages, styles, and practices which are employed in a field . . . conventional symbols used in map making and dictionaries, rules of social behavior, and rules, styles, or practices commonly employed in scholarly fields.

1.22 *Knowledge of trends and sequences*
Knowledge of the processes, directions, and movements of phenomena with respect to time—includes trends as attempts to point up the interrelationship among a number of specific events which are separated by time . . . also includes representations of processes which may involve time as well as causal interrelations of a series of specific events.

1.23 *Knowledge of classifications and categories*
Knowledge of the classes, sets, divisions, and arrangements which are regarded as fundamental or useful for a given subject field, purpose, argument, or problem.

1.24 *Knowledge of criteria*
Knowledge of the criteria by which facts, principles, opinions, and conduct are tested and judged.

1.25 *Knowledge of methodology*
Knowledge of the methods of inquiry, techniques, and procedures employed in a particular subject field as well as those employed in investigating particular problems and phenomena.

1.30 *Knowledge of the universals and abstractions in a field*
Knowledge of the major ideas, schemes, and patterns by which phenomena and ideas are organized . . . the large structures, theories, and generalizations which dominate a subject field . . .

1.31 *Knowledge of principles and generalizations*
Knowledge of particular abstractions which summarize observations of phenomena . . . the abstractions which are of greatest value in explaining, describing, predicting, or in determining the most appropriate and relevant action or direction to be taken.

1.32 *Knowledge of theories and structures*
Knowledge of the body of principles and generalizations together with their interrelations which present a clear, rounded, and systematic view of a complex phenomenon, problem, or field.

Programmers who read and discuss this work in relation to programming activity seemingly increase their recognition of the extent and variety of specific educational objectives. As they begin, moreover, to collect and order their own sets of objectives for their own particular units and groups of learners, they are more likely to achieve defensible positions and to be able to explain what they are doing.

Examples of Less Abstract Objectives

For a program entitled "Using Cloud Appearances to Predict the Weather," the programmer stipulated these specific objectives:

1. The student will understand that:
   (a) many people all over the earth look at the sky and wonder what the weather will be;
   (b) he can learn to tell of, or predict, the weather before it occurs;
   (c) he can predict the weather from the appearance of the clouds.
2. The following skills will be developed by the student:
   (a) he will identify specific cloud formations;
   (b) he will predict approaching weather when shown cloud formations;
   (c) he will use suitable vocabulary when discussing weather and clouds.
3. The following attitudes will be developed by the student:
   (a) he will demonstrate an openminded approach to the unknown and a technique for exploring it;
   (b) he will report accurately his success and failure in the use of cloud formations as weather predictors.

This program was designed for nine-, ten-, and eleven-year-old youngsters in the fourth, fifth, and sixth grades. One easily may discern that these three objectives lie at the more operational end of the ladder, and that they suggest an organization of materials that will function as a guide for the programmer. The first of these embraces substances characteristic of an introductory section. The second objective stresses the need for one series of items containing appropriate *panels* [7] on the identification of cloud formations, for another series on the kinds of weather that follow certain formations, and for special criteria to enable a learner to demonstrate that he can predict weather from cloud appearances. Under this objective, and perhaps

[7] A *panel* is a diagram, chart, or figure usually distinct from the items of a program.

throughout the entire program, the importance of exact terminology is apparent; precise vocabulary has to be used in a variety of contexts so that the young learners will begin to appreciate the value of accurate expression in dealing with knowledge and understanding. As to the third objective, it provides, almost automatically, experience for learners in meeting the challenges of everyday life and, perhaps, affords them an opportunity to taste both success and failure free from the ridicule of peers or others. This approach, of course, is only one of those that may be taken to solve the particular educational problem posed by the program's title. It is, however, an entirely reasonable one and illustrates how easily a programmer may proceed from a set of less abstract objectives to the actual direction and ordering of his program.

Consider now the sets of objectives formulated for three other programs constructed for use among elementary school pupils.

An Introduction to Entomology

The learner will know the following characteristics of insects [a list of the characteristics of insects was presented].

The learner will:

identify a living thing as an insect by counting to see that it has six legs and three body parts;

find and recognize both a compound eye and a simple eye on an insect specimen;

identify antennae on an insect specimen;

by examination of insect legs, suggest the type of movement an insect employs;

identify ovipositors on insect abdomen;

identify spiracles on the insect specimen;

read, spell, pronounce, and use correctly in meaningful conversation the term entomology.

Geometry for Sixth Graders

The learner will acquire a rudimentary knowledge of geometry and become more interested in arithmetic. To do so, he will:

identify 3-dimensional geometric shapes around him;

use meaningfully geometric vocabulary words such as prism, cylinder, sphere, pyramid, and cone;

distinguish between these shapes;

construct or find and label simple geometric shapes;

use the compass and protractor properly;

find volume of simple shapes like rectangle, prism, and cube.

How to Cross the Street Safely

To assure his preservation through an understanding of the best and safest way to cross a street, the learner will:

recognize a traffic light;

identify the three colors of the lights;

respond correctly to the commands of the lights;

describe the correct function of the traffic light in relation to pedestrian safety;

know about the safety patrol and its function;

react correctly to safety patrol and police direction at crossings;

cross streets at appropriate places and with regard to vehicular traffic.

Next, consider objectives for two programs to be used in the higher middle grades.

Sharing and Teamwork for Disturbed Children

For the teacher the objectives of the program will be perceived in terms of strengthened or altered values and attitudes. The learners should demonstrate discernible gains in the following areas. They will demonstrate:

less need for intervention by teachers, adults, or others to enforce or promote sharing and teamwork;

acceleration of the rate of progress in games and the amount of productivity in other group activities through fewer intrusions of problems resulting from imperfect concepts of sharing and teamwork;

an increase in motivation through the length of games and activities, through the frequency of requests for desired activity, or through the ease of undertaking a less desired activity.

Simple Machines

The learner will demonstrate the ability to:

recognize the three classes of levers as they appear in objects and in diagram form;

distinguish and name correctly the parts of a lever both in objects and in diagram form;

solve simple problems involving levers;

use correctly the technical vocabulary associated with levers;

recognize and utilize the practical advantages and limitations in the employment of levers.

Then there are these kinds of objectives in four programs intended for high school use.

Establishing Correct Verb Usage Patterns

To extinguish by repeated positive reinforcement of the right response certain common errors in verb usage, the learner will:

form correctly the simple present tense of all verbs;

form correctly all regular verbs and the irregular verbs *to see, to do, to come, to run,* in the simple past tense;

form correctly all regular verbs and the irregular verbs in the past perfect tense;

recognize and differentiate between the simple past tense and past perfect tense.

Tobacco, Alcohol, and Narcotics

The objectives of the program are:

to help the learner gain knowledge of contributions of narcotics and anesthetics to human welfare, and knowledge of the dangers of self-medication;

to recognize the effects of alcohol, tobacco, marijuana, and other narcotic drugs on the human organism and behavior, plus the reasons underlying their use;

to recognize the sociological and economic effects of the use of beverage alcohol;

to recognize the place of sound education and continued scientific research in solving the personal and social problems of intemperance.

Calculation of Molecular Weights

The learner will calculate correctly the molecular weight of any substance from its formula. He will:

select correct atomic weight for each element;

calculate the total weight of each element by use of the subscript;

calculate the total molecular weight of a substance from the sum of the atomic weights of its constituent elements.

Nouns

To identify nouns, the learner will:

designate nouns in a series of words;

distinguish nouns in a sentence;

use nouns correctly in writing sentences and phrases;

show in his oral expression that he understands nouns.

And, finally, there are these sets of objectives for five programs planned for use in higher education, industry, or both.

United Airlines Quick Reference Timetable

Overall objective: the learner will acquire a knowledge of and skill in the use of the Quick Reference Timetable (Q. R. T.) to quote specific information about flight schedules.

To establish an understanding of the contents and limitations of the Q. R. T. the learner will:

show that he knows and understands the basic format;

demonstrate knowledge of specific origin and destination information;

evince his understanding of the current date timetable;

recognize limitations of the Q. R. T. by its area concept, and its incomplete list of destinations.

To establish in the learner the ability to read pertinent flight information, he will:

realize that destination cities are listed alphabetically;

explain flight itineraries in local time;

locate and use reservation office telephone numbers at major cities listed;

quote correctly connecting flight information as shown in the Q. R. T.;

supply information about meals and class of service;

locate and use correctly the reference pages;

give airport location in relation to downtown area of city.

Matrix Arithmetic

The learner, upon completion of the program, will:

associate the word "matrix" with any size or shape of matrix;

construct any number of matrices of any size and shape;

use the specialized meaning of *row, column,* and *element* when applied to matrices;

give the number of the rows first and then the number of columns according to customary ways of describing the shape of a matrix, as in the example "B is a 5-row by 4-column matrix";

use the subscript notation to describe the position of an element in a matrix, as "*aij* is the element in the *i*th row and the *j*th column";

use capital letters to represent matrices and small letters to represent elements of matrices;

determine if two matrices are equal;

associate the phrase *row vector* with matrices that have exactly one row, and the phrase *column vector* with matrices that have exactly one column;

decide, if given two matrices, whether it is possible to add or subtract them;

add or subtract the matrices;

multiply a matrix by a number;

determine, if given two matrices and an order, whether it is possible to multiply them in that order;

determine the shape of the result of a permissible matrix multiplication without carrying out the multiplication.

Introduction to Practical Photography

To introduce photographic principles and to stimulate or encourage photographic skills by personal application and further study or instruction, the learner will:

use basic photographic terms and principles in such a way as to show that he recognizes them and understands their meanings;

obtain and use a camera to take pictures;

use instruction booklet for his particular camera in an efficient manner;

operate the camera to demonstrate a knowledge of the function of its parts;

discuss and ask intelligent questions about photography;

take additional instruction in photography.

The Grained Zinc Offset Lithographic Surface Plate

To achieve understanding of technical terms relative to lithographic platemaking, the learner will:

carry on discussions with journeymen platemakers;

direct surface platemaking operations;

estimate platemaking jobs taking into account potential problem areas.

To achieve familiarity with equipment and supplies necessary for surface platemaking, the learner will:

recognize platemaking equipment and supplies;

evaluate surface platemaking equipment;

select and procure proper and necessary supplies;

initiate remedial measures for inconsistencies of equipment.

To develop safe working practices, the learner will:

recognize all hazards connected with surface platemaking;

follow precautionary measures to avoid accidents;

react appropriately to any unsafe condition.

The Care of the Patient Having Radiation Therapy

To review briefly some concepts in cancer therapy necessary for an understanding of the present unit, the learner will:

demonstrate ability to use technical vocabulary adequate to clarify explanations given to patients, to read and comprehend literature in the field, and to converse knowledgeably with other members of the health team concerning the care of such patients;

differentiate between growth habits of benign and malignant tumors in order to understand the need for early treatment, and to accept the concept of radical treatment.

To gain basic knowledge about sources and effects of radiation, and the methods of delivering radiation to patients so as to plan and administer care to those undergoing such therapy, the learner will:

make treatment as tolerable as possible to the patient by helping him accept need for prolonged treatment, and by allaying his fears of the machinery used.

All these instances of objectives drawn from the efforts of neophyte programmers are neither distinguished examples of the goal-setting process nor the ideals among operational definitions. More precisely, they are good approximations of reasonable and adequate objectives constructed by individuals actively engaged in teaching. Invariably these teachers report that through such semantic manipulations they have acquired additional understanding and appreciation of what they have been teaching and programming.

The process, then, as well as the results, of preparing objectives for a particular instructional unit in terms of the desired behavior of the learners is an extremely useful experience to the novice preparing his first programs. What he gains is an appreciation of the power of operational definitions—the recognition, for instance, of specified behaviors toward which to program. He also acquires an awareness of the increased objectivity to be obtained from making abstract terms and words more concrete, and he enhances his understanding of the great variety of useful ways in which objectives may be stated. In addition, he finds an approach to the problem of selection of the more appropriate goals to suit the learner groups as well as the culture, and develops an orientation toward the organization, and necessary inclusions and exclusions, of the unit material to be programmed.

It should be noted that the present state of knowledge is such that we know little about the teaching of attitudes, values, and interests. Nevertheless, the programmer should be concerned about providing for students to develop a positive motivation toward instructional material. This can be done by seeing that appropriate contexts are used in the program sequence and that examples are timely, meaningful, understandable, and interesting to the students.

Finally, it becomes necessary to look at the objectives, as initially prepared, with relation to the criteria for unit selection and the assumptions made about the learners. Various questions can sharpen the skills of the programmer.

With regard to the criteria for selection of a unit, has there been a change in the unit as initially selected? For example, is it necessary to look again at such criteria as *ease, length,* and *logical order?*

Will a program building toward the defined goals be much more difficult than was originally thought?

Has development and expansion of the broad objectives changed the initial conception of the *length* of the program?

Have the priorities in the subject material been changed after *all* the goals were examined?

Have efforts to make broad objectives less abstract caused a re-alignment of criteria with respect to a changed purpose?

Does the development of specific aims suggest the need for another unit prior to the one originally selected?

With regard to the assumptions about the learners, has the validity of the assumptions about the learners been questioned by the operationally defined objectives? If so, do the assumptions have to be modified?

Was the diagnosis of the learner's ability—I.Q., past achievement, ratings of teachers or trainers—intensive enough? Or extensive enough?

Are the conclusions as to the age levels represented in the learner group such that the goals are realistic?

Do the less abstract and more concrete objectives lead to the conclusions that the goals chosen are the most desirable with regard to findings about the learner's socio-economic background?

Do the more complete objectives give more guidance in determining the appropriateness of the estimate of the learner's need for a change in attitudes, values, or interests?

Are the concrete objectives reachable in the learner's capacities to respond?

The idea as well as the process of interrelating the steps explored in Chapters 2 and 3 and in this one has stirred the imagination of many new programmers. As more of them begin to pursue this course, programs that are more suitable to the curricular needs of our society, programs that more learners will be able to utilize with profit, and programs that can be appraised more easily by potential users and, incidentally, more easily evaluated *after* use, can be expected to be forthcoming.

SELECTED READINGS

1. Bloom, Benjamin S., et al., *Taxonomy of Educational Objectives—The Classification of Educational Goals Handbook I: The Cognitive Domain,* New York: Longmans, Green, 1956.

A systematic and thorough classification of educational objectives. Also, a discussion of the classification problems.

2. Dale, Edgar, *Audio-Visual Methods in Teaching,* Revised Edition, New York: Henry Holt, 1959. Chapter IV, "The Cone of Experience."

An exposition of relationships between "direct experience" and "verbal symbols" (concrete to abstract) showing possibilities, in the context of audio-visual aids, for helping students learn.

3. French, Will, et al., *Behavioral Goals of General Education in High School,* New York: Russell Sage Foundation, 1957.

Results of a survey of general educational goals for high school carefully described and analyzed.

4. Kearney, Nolan C., *Elementary School Objectives,* New York: Russell Sage Foundation, 1953.

A collection of specific objectives of elementary education carefully outlined and evaluated.

5. Mager, Robert F., *Preparing Objectives for Programmed Instruction,* San Francisco: Fearon, 1962.

A guide to the preparation of behavioral objectives. This book should help the beginning programmer specify his objectives.

Chapter

Five

Selection of a Paradigm

"Whenever a student doesn't learn, it is not the fault of the student, but, rather that of the programmer," Arthur A. Lumsdaine, a pioneer in programmed learning, has written.[1] By asking the programmer to revise his program until it does work, he continued, "we can have many differences in approach and style, and still come out with a product which will be demonstrably better than any previous instruments that have been devised.

So far, the chapters of this book have paved the way for sitting down to the ardors of building a program. They have shown the potential programmer that the burden of success falls on his shoulders, not on the shoulders of the learners for whom his program is designed. The programmer now presumably knows the need for selecting a suitable unit for self-instruction; he knows further that he has to make assumptions about the learners and to choose objectives calculated to produce appropriate learning behaviors. One step remains to be considered before he can move on to the actual development and organization of program items. He must learn to adopt a *paradigm*—or model—to be followed scrupulously as he constructs his program.*

[1] Lumsdaine, Arthur A., in Lysaught, Jerome P. (Ed.), *Programmed Learning: Evolving Principles and Industrial Applications,* Ann Arbor, Mich.: Foundation for Research on Human Behavior, 1961, p. 38.

* A teacher who had taken the authors' courses in program construction told

The programming paradigm supplies the basic conceptual framework through which the individual items are connected. It is essential, therefore, that it be chosen in relation to the selection criteria, assumptions, and objectives. If the model employed complements the previous considerations, the actual writing of items will be simplified and the ultimate program will be more likely to conform to expectations.

There are many models from which to choose. They range from the entirely linear—or *extrinsic*—program at one extreme to a full branching—or *intrinsic*—program at the other. Between these lie an infinite number of varieties, but only a few major divisions need be investigated for the sake of illustration. For the inexperienced programmer, particularly, it is advisable to choose from these recognized groupings; as he gains confidence through practice he may perfect his own combination of models to carry out his objectives.

Linear or Extrinsic Programs

The linear, or extrinsic, programs present a sequential development of the material through which each student, regardless of his response, proceeds in exactly the same order. A diagram of the process would look like this:

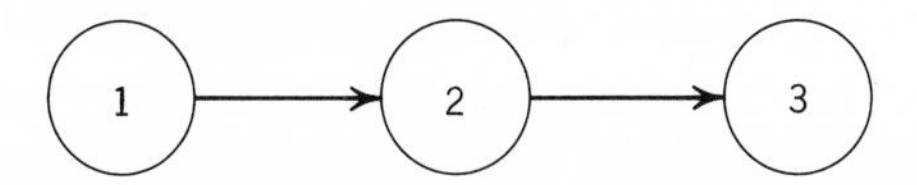

The student responds to the first item, and then, after receiving word of the accuracy and adequacy of his response, proceeds to the second item. He goes on to the third and subsequent items in linear form irrespective of any errors he might make on intervening items.

Typically the items are short. Sequences build through graduated development. Quite often the responses are con-

them some time after graduation that he quoted them repeatedly to school administrators. Flattered by the thought, one of the authors inquired what the former student said. "Well," he replied, "you once described programming as 'inspired drudgery' and that's exactly what it is."

structed by the student—that is, he is required to formulate and write out his own response to a stimulus. In the event that a student makes an incorrect response, the exposure of the correct one provides for immediate rectification. Later he will encounter sufficient items that review and restate the learning material to permit him to demonstrate correct response behavior to similar stimuli.[2]

A basic assumption of the linear program is that each stimulus should be designed to elicit the correct response by the student, and that his own construction of the responses is an integral part of the learning situation. In other words, the response is not a test to determine whether learning has taken place, but is an essential part of the learning itself. A corollary assumption is that responses made overtly—by constructing them in writing—more effectively assure the occurrence of learning.[3]

Figure 5-1 represents a typical sequence from a linear program.[4] The program "response" is shielded from the student until he has constructed his own response to the stimulus. Then he has the opportunity to compare the two.

The sample is indicative of the slow but steady progression of the linear program. At each step a little progress is made; ideally, each student should be equipped by the preceding items to make that progress. The emphasis of the linear program is to bring the student to the desired goal by means of a succession of these small steps so designed as to minimize errors and to provide a wide range of examples and conditions. Many programmers have found this paradigm to be a good first choice in starting to construct their material.

Since each learner will consider the same items in the same order as he pursues the program, there is a great responsibility on the programmer to develop an optimal unit which can be followed and mastered by virtually all students for whom it is intended. The program must be aimed at the lowest common denominator of his classroom population. He can draw comfort from the fact that students will vary considerably in the length

[2] In this regard it should be pointed out that Skinner's early teaching machines provided for a second display of items which the student missed.

[3] Krumboltz, John D., and Ronald Weisman, "The Effect of Overt vs. Covert Responding to Programmed Material," *Journ. of Educ. Psych.*, April, 1962.

[4] Holland, James G., and B. F. Skinner, *Analysis of Behavior*, New York: McGraw-Hill, 1961, pp. 41–45.

S-1.	Performing animals are sometimes trained with "rewards." The behavior of a hungry animal can be "rewarded" with ________.
R-1.	food
S-2.	A technical term for "reward" is reinforcement. To "reward" an organism with food is to ________ it with food.
R-2.	reinforce
S-3.	*Technically* speaking, a thirsty organism can be ________ with water.
R-3.	reinforced NOT rewarded
S-4.	The trainer reinforces the animal by giving it food ________ it has performed correctly.
R-4.	when, if, after
S-5.	Reinforcement and behavior occur in the temporal order: (1) ________, (2) ________.
R-5.	(1) behavior (2) reinforcement

Figure 5-1

of time consumed in following the program. Although the program is aimed for mastery by *all* his students, the superior ones will spend less time on it, generally, than will the slower learners.[5]

Conversational Chaining

A second paradigm for programming is that of conversational chaining. This was originated by John Barlow in the course of

[5] Holland, J. G., "Teaching Machines: An Application of Principles for the Laboratory" (Lumsdaine and Glaser, pp. 226–228).

experiments conducted in connection with the Earlham College Self-Instruction research project. Conversational chaining is closely related to the linear model, yet there are interesting differences between them.

Barlow became concerned over two aspects of the general linear model.[6] At the surface level, he was struck by the reactions of both students and teachers to the arrangement of a series of questions and answers. Although this series represents a sequence of stimuli and responses, all too often the initial reaction has been that, "this is a test!" The second area of his concern was more elemental. He pointed out that in building up a chain of responses, it is necessary first to bring student behavior under the control of a *discriminative stimulus;* then a new response can be reinforced by making the presentation of that stimulus contingent upon the emission of the second response. The process can be extended from there through a series of responses. Within the chain, each discriminative stimulus also functions as a reinforcer, and each reinforcer, in turn, serves as a discriminative stimulus. In comparing this behavioral model of a response chain to a programmed sequence of the linear type, Barlow observed that discrete question-answer pairs did not reflect the chaining aspect as closely as they should.

To meet his two objectives—for an avoidance of a format that closely resembled a test, and for a closer analogy between the program and a behavioral response chain—he constructed another kind of paradigm. In graphic form, it looks like this:

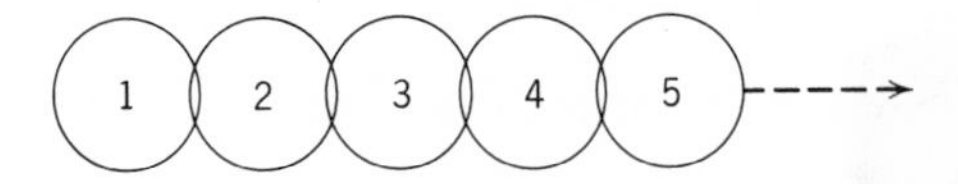

Each item is connected to the succeeding item, and the response to the second item, for instance, becomes a part of the stimulus of the third, and so on down the line.

Figure 5-2 exemplifies a program of this type.[7]

Several important resemblances between the conversational

[6] Barlow, John A., "Conversational Chaining in Teaching Machine Programs," Richmond, Ind.: Earlham College, 1960, mimeo. (See also the article by the same name in *Psychol. Rep.,* **8:**207–209, 1960.)

[7] *Ibid.*

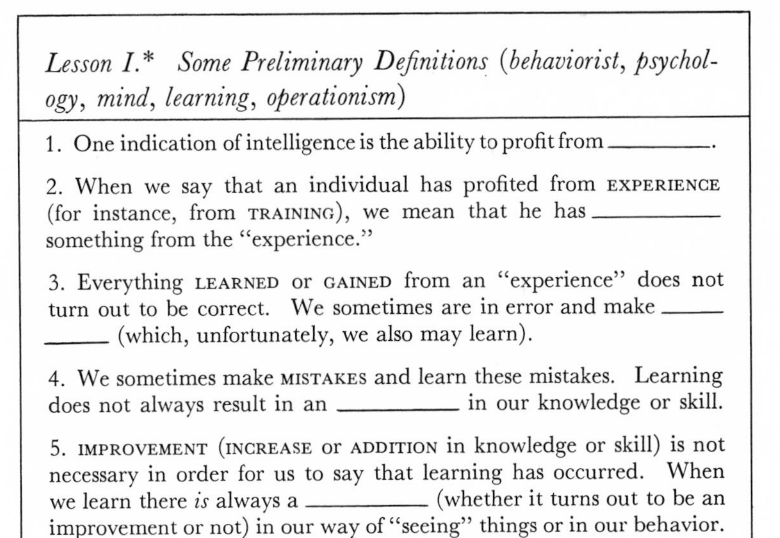
Lesson I. Some Preliminary Definitions (behaviorist, psychology, mind, learning, operationism)*

1. One indication of intelligence is the ability to profit from ________.

2. When we say that an individual has profited from EXPERIENCE (for instance, from TRAINING), we mean that he has ________ something from the "experience."

3. Everything LEARNED or GAINED from an "experience" does not turn out to be correct. We sometimes are in error and make ______ ______ (which, unfortunately, we also may learn).

4. We sometimes make MISTAKES and learn these mistakes. Learning does not always result in an ________ in our knowledge or skill.

5. IMPROVEMENT (INCREASE or ADDITION in knowledge or skill) is not necessary in order for us to say that learning has occurred. When we learn there *is* always a ________ (whether it turns out to be an improvement or not) in our way of "seeing" things or in our behavior.

Figure 5-2

* In the subsequent development of this technique Barlow has made some slight changes in presentation, but the principle remains unchanged.

chain program and the linear program are evident. The student goes through each item in the chain in a strict sequence as ordered by the programmer. Also, the student is required to construct his response for each step. He receives information about his response by moving on to the next item. The program response, however, is contained within the context of the next stimulus. By glancing at the capitalized word or words, which serve as the correct response for the preceding item, the student can readily confirm the correctness of his last previous response, and continue reading the stimulus.

Barlow believed that the conversational nature of the program would keep the student involved and moving along from item to item throughout the unit better than if the material were cut distinctly into paired stimulus-response bits. Hopefully, the unit would assume a greater continuity, and the student would be aided toward an integrated understanding of the lesson.

For the same purpose of continuity the brief statement is made, preceding the first item, about the aim of the lesson as a whole. This is designed to give the student an objective in undertaking the unit, and to provide a terminal point at which he will have knowingly met his objectives.

The very requirement of interlocking the items necessitates a certain amount of repetition in each item in order to tie it back rationally to its predecessor, and, in addition, to make the program as a whole proceed deliberately without sudden leaps or elisions. As a result, conversational chaining is a good paradigm for newcomers to choose.

Modified Linear Programs

Both conversational chaining and strict linear programming compel each student to progress through the learning material according to its set order. Both approaches also are designed to produce student mastery for those learners who fall within the limits of the programmer's assumptions. This, necessarily, raises problems of individual learning behavior. Slow learners can achieve mastery only if the program includes a great number of review and repetitive items. Some of these, it is true, may be necessary also for the faster learners, but it is reasonable to expect that what may be vital review for some students becomes tedious redundancy to others.

The programmer can handle this kind of problem in the linear program by accepting the fact that some students will receive excessive review, but will move rapidly at their optimum individual rate, and will not be particularly bothered by redundant items. He also can reduce the number of review items by requiring the students to rework items on which they erred. This means that learners who do errorless work will not be required to do as much review and repetition, and that the total number of review items can be trimmed down. Or he can attempt to vary continually the context of review material by placing it in differing structures, conditions, and relationships so as to avoid as much as possible the development of redundancy and tedium. The last of these methods is useful at all times.

Nevertheless, there may be cases of considerable differences among students, or cases in which the subject matter—for instance, English grammar or mathematics—requires so much review for slower learners that it approximates a form of drill. Under such conditions, another alternative may be desirable for the faster learners. This would consist of modifying the linear program to allow for skipping certain review sequences when responses have been accurate. A diagram of such a program looks like this:

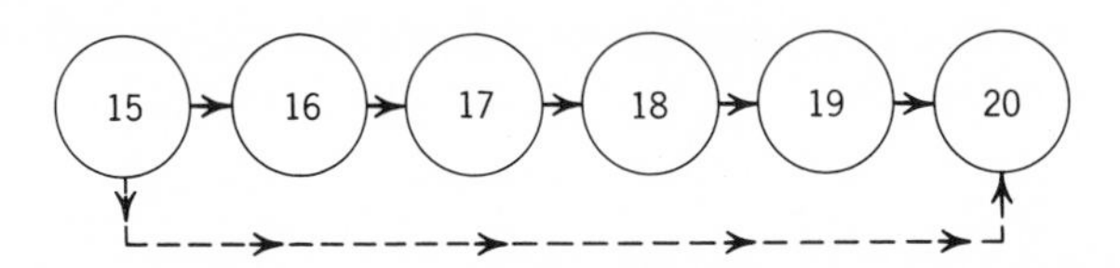

In this instance, item 15 might appear as in Figure 5-3.

The item functions as the termination of a developmental sequence. If the student has mastered the skills previously taught, he will not need additional review at this point. On the other hand, if there is still some difficulty apparent, items 16–19 can serve as a review and skill exercise. Those students who need additional aid continue on through the linear program; those who demonstrate mastery can skip to the next instructional sequence.

Although this modification of the linear program provides for students who can learn effectively without all the review

15. *Cas tle* is divided this way. Divide these words:

waddle candle
sable trouble

15. wad dle sa ble
can dle trou ble

If your response is entirely correct, go on to item 20. If you made one or more errors go to item 16.

Figure 5-3

items constructed for the slow learner, it is conceivable that the reverse variation also could be used effectively. That is, the student who reaches the nineteenth item and still cannot break selected words into proper syllables might be directed to return to the first item and redo the entire sequence—not just those particular items on which he erred. If the sequence is truly developmental, this would certainly seem preferable to his working solely on isolated items.

Linear Programs with Sub-linears

The modified form of linear programming utilizing the skipping technique, as we have seen, aids in handling problems of review and over-review. By reversing the skipping procedure, moreover, the linear sequence may be used as a form of remedial instruction for those students who do not achieve mastery on their first journey through the items. Another aspect of student learning, however, invites the application of still another paradigm. Rapid learners often will desire additional material to enrich themselves, and particularly information to supplement their understanding of the knowledge or skill they are developing in the programmed sequence. As individual learning rates vary on programmed material, it is fairly simple to introduce enrichment elements in the form of linear sub-programs which may be taken at the option of the student—or not taken if interest or time is lacking. The diagram of such a program would look like this:

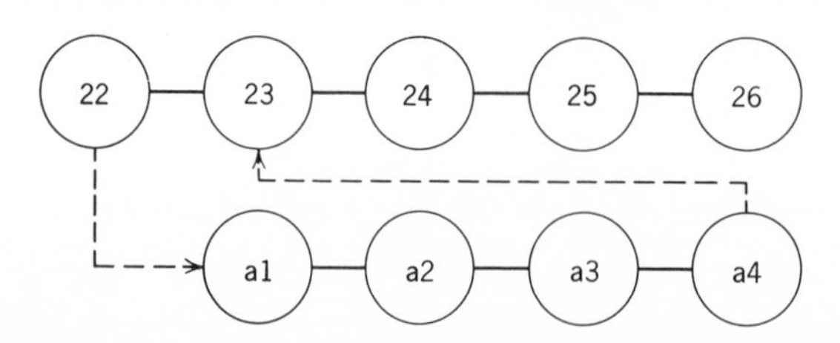

Item 22 of the main linear program might read in the form of Figure 5-4.

Students who desire the additional information can take the

22. The circumference of a circle is equal to π times the ________ of the circle.

22. diameter

As you know, π is an approximate number. If you want an *extra* look at a closer approximation to π go to item a-1. If not, go on to item 23.

Figure 5-4

side trip through the linear sub-program a-1, a-2, a-3, and a-4. Later they would return to the main line program. Indeed, there are other ways of adding enrichment experiences for students. For instance, an entire program, directly or tangentially related to the original program, might constitute an enrichment exercise for those who wished to take it.

Linear Programs with Criterion Frames

The final linear programming paradigm to be considered here has relevance when the assumptions about the learners include the fact that different levels of preparation are to be found among them relative to the learning objectives. In such a situation, certain *frames*—or items—called criterion or test frames may be used to direct the students along linear paths according to their responses at these critical junctures.

Criterion frames are not to be confused with those frames that terminate a sequence. A terminal frame is designed to permit a student to demonstrate his mastery of that sequence. A criterion frame, however, is used to determine whether the student should go through a particular sequence. For instance, a program in physics or mathematics might include a sequence on the transliteration of the Greek and English alphabets. In the assumptions, the programmer recognizes that some students will have had prior instruction in, and acquaintance with, the Greek alphabet, whereas others will not. A programming model can be developed on this basis:

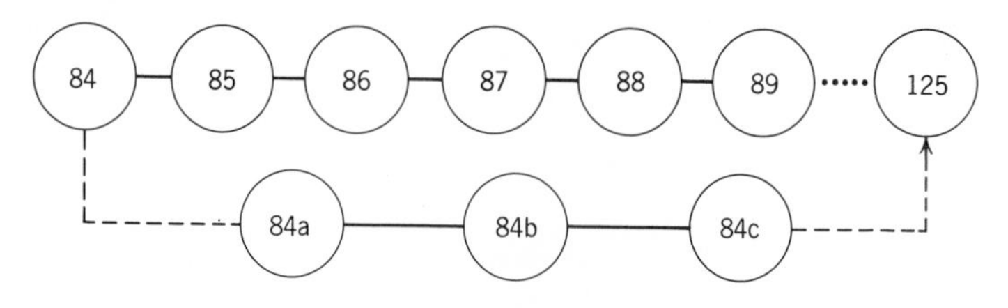

Item 84 might appear as in Figure 5-5.

The illustrated item would begin a programmed development on the Greek alphabet; item 84a simply might be another criterion frame designed to see whether the student understands additional letters of the alphabet. Items 84b and 84c could call for additional knowledge to be demonstrated. If the student showed mastery on all criterion items, he would be directed into the linear mainstream at a point following the end of the sequence on the Greek alphabet, say item 125. The criterion frames showed that he need not concern himself with a certain portion of the programmed material.

Criterion frames also may be used to assign students to various program *tracks* in the linear style. If, for instance, there are two linear programs on quadratic equations–one for students with

84. Let's see if you have had some experience with the Greek alphabet. Write out the first five letters of that alphabet in proper order—use Greek letters and equivalent English spellings. (small letters, not caps)

84. alpha—α
beta—β
gamma—γ
delta—δ
epsilon—ϵ

If right, go on to item 84a. If you made an error, or if you are not sure of Greek letters, go to item 85.

Figure 5-5

an excellent mathematics background, and the other, containing many more developmental and review items, for students not as well prepared—criterion frames help the students to pick the track best suited to each.

Intrinsic Programming

All the programming paradigms examined thus far essentially have been variations of the basic linear program developed by B. F. Skinner. In most cases, the special features or arrangements of the models were designed to cope with particular problems of individual students—problems of review, remedy, or enrichment—and differences in programmer choice and subject matter requirements. There is another philosophic approach to paradigms that has similar concerns, but different solutions to suggest. This other approach is that of intrinsic programming—known familiarly as the branching form of program construction.

Norman Crowder developed intrinsic programming from his experiences over several years in training armed forces personnel to understand and use complex electronic equipment. Crowder explained his basic approach in this way: [8] The student is given the material to be learned in small logical units; immediately after he has read and digested one of these units, he is given a short test on it; the results of the test are used to determine what next unit of information shall be presented to the student. For instance, the student's response to a test item might indicate that he has understood the lesson unit thoroughly and is ready to go to the next piece of information. On the other hand, his test response may indicate that he does not understand the information he has just studied, or it may show that he has understood the lesson material only partially. In either case, he would be directed through the medium of the program to the next appropriate bit of information—to restate the lesson, or to clarify a point that he has misunderstood, or to return to the previous unit of material and work through it again.

[8] Crowder, Norman A., "Automatic Tutoring by Intrinsic Programming" (Lumsdaine and Glaser, pp. 286–298).

The intrinsic programming model is designed, through interaction with the student, to present him with adaptive, tutorial instruction based on his previous responses rather than to inform him simply of the correctness or incorrectness of his replies. A diagram of a simple step in an intrinsic program looks like this:

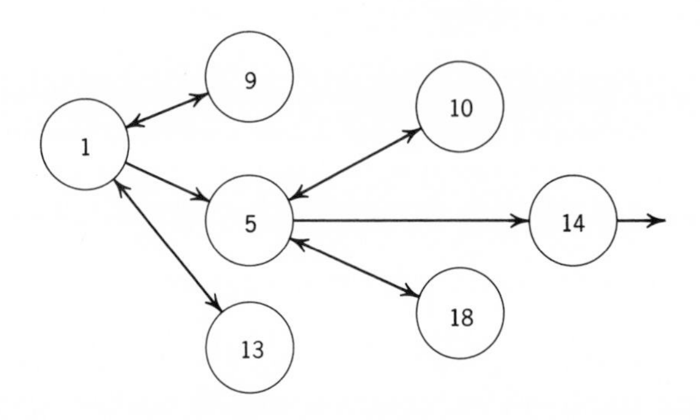

At the first item, the student is given a small unit of information —in this case about bases and exponents. He is then given a brief test question on the material and a choice of three responses. If he selects the correct answer, he is referred to the fifth item and goes on to the next instructional unit. If his reply to the first test question is incorrect or inadequate, he is sent to either the ninth or the thirteenth item where he gets additional information, and is then returned to the first item to take the test again. Having gotten to the fifth item directly, or after intermediate stops, he reads another unit and answers another test question which will direct him to the tenth, fourteenth, or eighteenth item depending on the accuracy and completeness of his response.

To illustrate how this is done in practice, here are sample items from the diagrammed sequence: [9]

[9] Crowder, Norman A., "A Sample Sequence from the Tutortext on the Arithmetic of Computers," Goleta, Calif.: U.S. Industries, Inc., 1960.

Page 1

We have defined the symbol b^n as meaning "the product reached by using the number b as a factor n times." Thus, for example:

$$2^3 = 2 \times 2 \times 2 = 8$$

$$3^2 = 3 \times 3 = 9$$

$$b^2 = b \times b$$

etc.

We have also learned that in an expression of the form b^n, the number b is called the *base* and the number n is called the *exponent*.

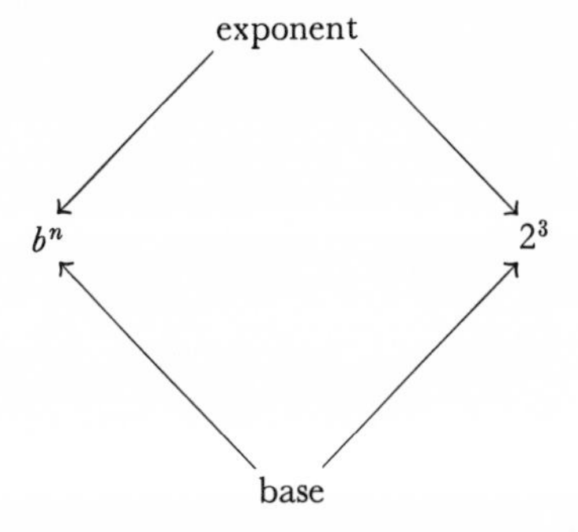

Finally, we have seen that a number expression such as 2^3 is called "the 3rd power of 2" or "2 raised to the 3rd power," and so on.

Now here is a question on this review material. Pick an answer and turn to the page number given after the answer you choose. The question is:

If the base of an expression is 2, and the exponent is 3, what is the expression equal to?

Answer	*Page*
8	5
9	9
I have no idea.	13

(from Page 1) Page 13

Your answer was: I have no idea.

Well, let's see if we can explain a little more fully.

Some of the numbers in our number system are the products of factors. The number 15, for example, is the product of the numbers 5 and 3. That is, $5 \times 3 = 15$. The numbers 5 and 3 are called "factors" of 15.

Now there are some numbers that are the product of the *same* factor used a certain number of times. The number 16, for instance, is the product of the number 4 used as a factor twice. $4 \times 4 = 16$. A number that is the product of the *same* factor used a certain number of times can be written in the form b^n, where b is called the *base* and represents the number that is used as a factor and n is called the *exponent* and tells the number of times the base is to be used as a factor. So the number 16 written in the form b^n would be 4^2. 4^2 means "4 used as a factor twice," or

$$4^2 = 4 \times 4 = 16.$$

Now, the question on page 1 stated that the base, b, of the expression is 2 and the exponent, n, is 3. If we substitute these values in the expression b^n, we have

$$b^n = 2^3.$$

2^3, of course, means that 2 is to be used as a factor 3 times. So

$$2^3 = 2 \times 2 \times 2.$$

And what is 2 × [illegible]l to?

Return to page 1 and choose the correct answer.

(from Page 1) Page 5

Your answer was: If the base of an expression is 2 and the exponent is 3, then the expression is equal to 8.

You are correct. $2^3 = 2 \times 2 \times 2 = 8$.

Very well. Now, to continue this quick review, you may have learned previously that if b^m and b^n are two powers of the same base, then there is a short-cut way of multiplying these two numbers, as shown below.

$$(b^m)(b^n) = b^{(m+n)}$$

Thus $$(2^3)(2^5) = 2^{(3+5)} = 2^8$$

and $$(4^2)(4^3) = 4^{(2+3)} = 4^5, \text{ etc.}$$

Also, there is a similar rule for a division involving two powers of the same base.

$$\frac{b^m}{b^n} = b^{(m-n)}$$

Thus $$\frac{5^6}{5^4} = 5^{(6-4)} = 5^2$$

and $$\frac{7^3}{7^2} = 7^{(3-2)} = 7^1, \text{ etc.}$$

These "formulas" were justified at so[illegible]ngth in the full text of The Arithmetic of Computers. Here [illegible]erely state them and hurry on to get to the interesting p[illegible] be sure you have understood what has been said up[illegible]at is the result of dividing 8^6 by 8^2?

Answer

$\frac{8^6}{8^2} = 8^{(\frac{6}{2})} = 8^3$ [illegible]

$\frac{8^6}{8^2} = 8^{(6-2)} = 8^4$ 14

I don't know. 18

(from Page 1) Page 9

Your answer was: If the base of an expression is 2 and the exponent is 3, then the expression is equal to 9.

You have it backwards. You used the number 3 as the base and 2 as the exponent, and we want it the other way around.

In our brief discussion on page 1, we stated that in the expression b^n the number b was the *base*, the number to be used as a factor, and that the number n was the *exponent*, which tells the number of times the base is to be used as a factor. So if the base is 2 and the exponent is 3, and we substitute these values in the expression b^n, we have 2^3.

Now, 2^3 means the product reached by using the number 2 as a factor 3 times.

And what is "2 used as a factor 3 times" equal to?

Return to page 1 and choose the correct answer.

There are obvious surface differences between the intrinsic programming model and the extrinsic models considered previously. One of the most apparent is that the intrinsic program involves multiple-choice responses while most extrinsic, or linear, programs rely on constructed responses by the student. In itself, this is not as great a difference as it may seem. Linear programs can make use of multiple-choice responses and do in sequences involving stimulus discrimination—and even in such items as *will* or *will not, larger than* or *smaller than,* to which the student must respond by selecting the assertion that best completes the program step. Correspondingly, intrinsic test questions can demand a constructed response—prior to the selection of the alternative. For example: Q: $4.23 \times 8.14 =$

(a) 34.44 (b) 34.43 (c) 34.34

A student would have to multiply the numbers completely before he could make anything but a wild guess.

Another difference between the two general programming models is this: in most cases, students using linear programs will proceed to a subsequent item *regardless* of the correctness or incorrectness of their responses; in intrinsic programs, the student will be directed to diverse items *as a result* of the correctness or incorrectness of his response.

This manner of handling student responses cuts to the heart of the difference between extrinsic and intrinsic programming.

Linear programs are designed to utilize the student response as an integral part of the learning sequence, and do not provide for learning from the program without the active response and its consequent reinforcement. In intrinsic programming, a different assumption prevails. Here it is assumed that the student will learn material from the program because it is carefully broken down into logically ordered steps. Student response, therefore, primarily becomes a diagnostic tool rather than a learning device. The response indicates the completeness and accuracy of the student's covert learning. This essential distinction is one to be kept in mind in considering the various paradigms.

Intrinsic programs have been developed in many subject-matter fields, including mathematics, electronics, law, and contract bridge. Although the intrinsic model would seem to be pertinent to a wide range of programmed units, it has particular appeal for programmers in an area where constant decision-making is required. Since the intrinsic paradigm stresses testing and decision making, there is a surface relationship to the program objectives of units on such things as field testing, trouble shooting, or diagnosis.

A fairly common assumption made by inexperienced programmers is that intrinsic programs are easier to construct because they permit the development and use of larger steps in their items. Actually, this form of programming is more demanding in other respects. Intrinsic programs require adequate provision for those who do not learn successfully on initial test material. This means better understanding of possible problems, and the construction of analytical test items that truly will discriminate between full understanding, some lesser knowledge, and no knowledge at all. Perhaps the safest assumption to make is that linear *and* intrinsic programs impose equal demands for skill on the part of the programmer, but that requirement of a particular skill may vary somewhat depending on the general kind of program being constructed.

Full Branching Programs

Crowder and other programmers who work with intrinsic paradigms stress the complexity of the adaptive system, which can be manipulated to meet student needs. Most of the published intrinsic programs, however, use only a simple branching technique. If an item has four alternatives, the student will find one that leads him on through the program, whereas the other three choices usually return him—with some additional information—to the starting point with the injunction to choose another answer.

Most attempts to create programming paradigms that are adaptive to student learning behavior, whether the basic program is linear or intrinsic, eventually result in a computer-like device, which incorporates memory systems and analytical response capabilities. Such a system permits analysis of student response, and the arrangement of future learning contingencies in the light of that response. As noted, the full branching program can use either linear or intrinsic material, but it requires mechanical means of analysis and presentation.

In addition to the papers by Crowder on the possibilities of full branching programs,[10] other research reports on experimental projects using computer-based systems have been prepared by programmers at IBM,[11] and at Massachusetts Institute of Technology.[12] In both latter cases adaptive procedures were given maximum play by computers to permit the use of full branching paradigms.

Random Effects of Various Paradigms

The choice of a programming paradigm will have an important influence on the construction of a programmed sequence. As has been pointed out, most linear programs treat the response activity of the student as an integral portion of the learning process. This in turn necessitates an inherent pace of gradual development in such programs. Because intrinsic programs include the response as a diagnostic tool, the learning rate may be

[10] Crowder, Norman A., "Automatic Tutoring by Intrinsic Programming" (Lumsdaine and Glaser, pp. 289–298).

[11] Rath, Gustave, Nancy Anderson, and R. C. Brainerd, "The IBM Research Center Teaching Machine Project" (Galanter, pp. 117–130).

[12] "IBM 709 Tutors M.I.T. Students," *AID*, November, 1961, p. 67.

accelerated in them. However, the analysis of error becomes even more important.

Another impact of various paradigms is on the handling of individual learning differences. In some cases, sub-programs for enrichment, or skipping for avoidance of unnecessary review passages, or conversational chaining for heightened integration may be indicated. Or the programmer may wish to use combinations—or variations—of several paradigms as he advances from unit to unit.

A frequent question heard is, "How do these paradigms compare in effectiveness?" The person posing the question usually goes on to ask, "Are there comparative results for a program in algebra using a linear style, and one using the intrinsic model?" Some preliminary studies have been undertaken [13] and while the findings are interesting and, perhaps, suggestive of further research, most programmers would agree that more experimentation will be necessary before anyone can speak with true authority on the relative merits of various paradigms.[14]

It is sufficient to point out that each of these paradigms has been used effectively in preparing programmed units for use in a teaching situation. For the teacher it becomes a matter of matching selection, assumptions, and objectives to a desirable model.

Paradigm Selection and the Programming Process

The last step in programming before starting to order and construct items is the selection of a paradigm. The preceding pages have presented several models which embrace a wide range of programming approaches. It is important, however, always

[13] Coulson, John E., and Harry W. Silberman, "Effects of Three Variables in a Teaching Machine," *Journ. of Educ. Psych.,* 51:135–43, June, 1960. Fry, Edward B., "A Study of Teaching Machine Response Modes" (Lumsdaine and Glaser, pp. 469–474). Roe, Arnold, et al., "Automated Teaching Methods Using Linear Programs," Report No. 60-105, Los Angeles: Department of Engineering, University of California, December, 1960.

[14] Krumboltz, John D., "Meaningful Learning and Retention: Practice and Reinforcement Variables," *Rev. of Educ. Res.,* Vol. XXXI, No. 5, December, 1961, pp. 535–546.

to select the programming paradigm on the basis of the unit involved, the learners to be accommodated, and the objectives to be achieved. In other words, the paradigm must be linked to the earlier steps in the programming process. Perhaps the way to illustrate this is by raising a number of questions that relate the paradigm to the previous programming steps.

With respect to the selection of a unit, does the unit involve an ascending order of complex skills which must be closely interrelated? If so, perhaps a linear program might be best to start. Does the unit involve discrimination or selection? If so, an intrinsic model may be the best choice. If the unit is to be inserted into an over-all educational experience, can the paradigm assist the total situation as well as present the program successfully?

With regard to the assumptions about the learners, are they evenly matched on going into the unit? If so, little individual adaptive work may be necessary and a linear program may handle all students successfully. Is individual ability highly variable? If so, intrinsic material, or skipping techniques, or criterion frames may be desirable. Are the learners experienced in this subject? If so, a programming model which allows faster development may be preferred. If not, a gradual development may be indicated. Are the learners experienced with programmed materials? If so, more complicated directions may be followed, and the programmer may wish to change the model simply for the sake of variety.

With regard to the objectives of the instruction, do they require overt response, or will covert learning be acceptable? How important is the difference between developing response behavior and developing discriminative or selective behavior? Does one of the programming models approximate in its design the ultimate behavior sought in the student? How gradual or rapid a development of the material is consistent with the objectives of the unit?

These questions indicate the areas to be explored in the selection of an appropriate paradigm. There is consolation in the fact that a programmer can bend almost any paradigm to his purpose. Nevertheless, when he considers his unit, his students, and his objectives, as well as related aspects of review, remedy, and enrichment, he may find that one or two programming models seem most appropriate. As he gains greater experience and proficiency in the art of programming, he will develop greater facility in matching a model to his selected unit of instruction.

SELECTED READINGS

1. Barlow, John A., "Conversational Chaining in Teaching Machine Programs," Richmond, Ind.: Earlham College Self-Instructional Program, 1960, mimeo. (See also the article by the same name in *Psychol. Rep.*, **8**:207–209, 1960.)

This is the only description to our knowledge of the conversational chaining paradigm for programming. Barlow's description of it, and his reflections on other models for programming, are helpful to the beginning programmer.

2. Galanter, Eugene (Ed.), *Automatic Teaching: The State of the Art,* New York: John Wiley and Sons, 1959.

   Beck, Jacob, "On Some Methods of Programming," pp. 55–62.

   Skinner, B. F., "The Programming of Verbal Knowledge," pp. 63–68.

General considerations of the models to be used in programming instructional sequences.

3. Holland, James G., and B. F. Skinner, *The Analysis of Behavior,* New York: McGraw-Hill, 1961.

The model program for linear sequences. This is well worth study as a carefully written and revised effort.

4. Lumsdaine, Arthur A., and Robert Glaser (Eds.), *Teaching Machines and Programmed Learning: A Source Book,* Washington, D.C.: NEA, 1960.

   Crowder, Norman A., "Automatic Tutoring by Intrinsic Programming," pp. 286–298.

   Fry, Edward B., "A Study of Teaching Machine Response Modes," pp. 469–474.

Crowder, of course, is the originator of intrinsic programming, and his article explains that paradigm. Fry's study is one of the first comparative examinations of programming models.

5. Lysaught, Jerome P. (Ed.), *Programmed Learning: Evolving Principles and Industrial Applications,* Ann Arbor, Mich.: Found. for Research on Human Behavior, 1961.

   Lumsdaine, Arthur A., "Some Differences in Approach to the Programming of Instruction," pp. 37–52.

   Skinner, B. F., "Learning Theory and Future Research," pp. 59–66.

These two articles provide a brief overview of various programming models and their significance to learning.

Chapter Six

Constructing the Program

The preliminaries have been completed. A unit has been selected for programming. Assumptions have been made about the learners. The learning objectives have been stated in relation to the behaviors desired. A program paradigm has been chosen. Now it is time for the main engagement, the construction of a programmed sequence. Before commencing to build the program item by item, however, some thought should be expended on the order or arrangement of the sequence. By planning the sequencing beforehand, the writing of the items becomes a lighter task, and the eventual editing and review are buttressed by a stronger rationale for checking what has been done.

Methods for Ordering Items

As a matter of fact, the preliminary exercises already have foreshadowed some of the factors of sequencing the items. In selecting the unit to be programmed, for instance, its relation to the units that precede and follow it have been considered. From making assumptions about the consumers of the program emerged the need for a starting point for the material. Similarly, the operational objectives gave birth to the ultimate aims of the programmed effort; when the objectives are stated in great de tail, they in themselves might be a sufficient guide to the sequencing of items.

More likely, however, the new programmer will need further assistance. Several methods may be suggested for ordering, or sequencing, program items in a manner that proceeds easily and directly to the instructional goals.

THE PRAGMATIC APPROACH. This method, developed from experience with classroom teachers who were learning to program, depends on the alignment of the behavioral aims into a logical order—logical on the basis of the programmer's selection, assumptions, and objectives. This order is then examined for its internal logic and "flow" from beginning to end. For example, the first several objectives for a program in *matrix algebra,* as we have seen, desire that the student upon completion of the program will use and associate the word *matrix* with any size or shape matrix; construct any number of matrices of any size and shape; apply the specialized meaning of *row, column,* and *element* to matrices correctly; and use the convention of giving the number of rows first and then the number of columns, in describing a matrix—as B is a 5×4 matrix.[1] Since these objectives fractionate the learning process, and represent the order of the learnings as well as the terminology that the programmer wishes to impart, they become a sequential guide to be followed in the construction of items.

Many times, however, the programmer will wish to develop from his objectives an outline of the steps that will compose that behavior. In other words, he may have to add detailed information to explain how to reach his objective. An objective cited by one programmer was that his "subjects will interpret data recorded on IBM cards by the twelve-channel code." To sequence the items to meet that objective, he began by implementing his original outline.

To interpret IBM card data, he noted, the subject must learn that data is recorded on IBM cards by means of punched holes; also that punching takes place in two main areas, the lower, or numerical, section and the upper, or zone, section. He must learn, in addition, that the numerical section is further divided into 10 horizontal rows, one for each digit 0 to 9, and that the

[1] See Chapter 4, p. 65.

zone section is divided into 3 horizontal rows, 0, 11, and 12; the zero row is common to both zone and numerical sections. Besides all this, he must learn that punched holes can be identified as characters—that is, digits, letters of the alphabet, and special symbols, such as #, $, %, &, etc.—and that 80 characters can be punched in one IBM card. . . .

This example suffices to demonstrate that sequencing demands specific and detailed outlining of the program's objectives. If these objectives are fully fractionated, sequencing becomes almost self-evident. If the sequencing possibilities are *not* seen readily, further break-down of the objectives may be necessary.

Because they are integral parts of a studied outline of the material, it is imperative to list the terminology, objects, and materials, all of which the student will meet for the first time since these, too, must be incorporated into the program. It is important also to review the sequential outline continually as items are written and revised or rearranged, if it becomes obvious that responses in the program preferably should be made in a different order. Nevertheless, the outline provides a conceptual direction to the sequencing of items, and is some guarantee against the omission of important information as the program is written.

THE RULEG SYSTEM. A different approach to organizing the sequence of programmed items is suggested in a paper describing the RULEG system.[2] The basis for this method is an assumption that material to be presented in a program consists of either rules (RU) or examples (EG). The first step is to state the aims of the program. Then, as many rules (RU) as possible that relate to the determined behavior are listed. By using outside resources including subject-matter experts, the list of rules is completed and examples (EG) of each rule are collected. A logical sequence of the rules in the order of learning, together with appropriate examples, is fashioned. This is followed by a finer sequence of the rules developed from a so-called RU *matrix* which is a graphic representation of the relationships between, and among, all the rules included in the goal. The matrix is

[2] Evans, James, Robert Glaser, and Lloyd Homme, "The RULEG System for the Construction of Programmed Verbal Learning Sequences," Department of Psychology, University of Pittsburgh, 1960.

Squaring Two-Digit Numbers Ending in 5 *

Frame	Answer	
1. To SQUARE a number, multiply it by itself. Example: To square 3, multiply 3 times 3. The answer is 9. Also: To square 6, multiply 6 times 6. The answer is _____.	36	
2. The square of 8 is: 8 times 8, or 64. The square of 5 is: 5 times 5, or _____.	25	
3. The square of 7 is 49. The square of 3 is _____.	9	
4. The square of 4 is _____.	16	
5. When you count, the number that comes next after a number is called the FOLLOWER of that number. The follower of 4 is 5. The follower of 6 is 7. The follower of 8 is _____.	9	

Figure 6-1

* James L. Evans, Teaching Machines, Inc., 1960.

filled with examples of the various rules, and the final order is arranged by inspection of the matrix and the relationships indicated by its form. The frames then may be written, usually in the form of stating the rule, followed by a complete example of the rule and an incomplete example of the rule which the student must finish.

Programmers interested in exploring this approach in greater detail will find a more elaborate explanation of this system elsewhere.[3] Certainly, it is an appropriate companion to the pragmatic approach. As both systems begin with a statement of terminal behavior, it becomes a matter of individual preference

[3] *Ibid.*

and operational ease as to which is to be employed in the ordering of the learning materials.

If the materials are collected in the form of rules and examples, however, the programmer may find interesting variations in arrangement. It is quite conceivable, for instance, that an inductive learning program can be developed out of a series of examples from which the student composes his own formulation of the appropriate rule.

Figure 6-1 illustrates a RULEG sequence.

THE MATHETICS SYSTEM. Another analytic vehicle for the ordering and sequencing of program items has been described by Thomas Gilbert. He has sought to apply systematically the principles of reinforcement theory to the analysis and reconstruction of learning, and has developed a complex system called *mathetics* for organizing and sequencing a learning program.[4] Although mathetics is too involved for detailed discussion in this book, the programmer who wishes to know more about it can find an explanation together with examples and sample program sequences in Gilbert's account of the method.

Briefly, the first step in the mathetics system is the writing of a *prescription*. This is a description of the behaviors that constitute mastery in a given subject-matter area. The prescription is followed by the development of a *domain theory* which consists of listing the essential elements of the subject matter in behavioral terms. Next, an *analytic repertory* is constructed to describe the observations of a *subject-matter master*.

A *characterization* is now prepared—that is to say, a description of the generalizations to be taught, of the competition in present behavior that exists with adequate performance, and of the behavior available to overcome that competition. Finally, an *exercise design* is devised in a sequence consistent with the characterization.

One of the more interesting aspects of the mathetics system is in the rationale of its sequencing. A number of learning operations are presented in reverse order to the customary way of teaching. For instance, the first item in a sequence on long

[4] Gilbert, Thomas F., "Mathetics: The Technology of Education, I. The General System," New York: TOR Education, Inc., 1961, mimeo.

division requires the student to obtain the remainder, the previous steps of the problem having been properly performed and shown in the program. Each item requires the student to do one prior operation in the process of long division until, when he reaches the terminal step of the sequence, he performs the entire process.

This backward process is adapted from Gilbert's analysis of animal learning behavior. It is designed to provide the greatest reinforcement—in this case, the effect of having completed the last step in the process of long division—and then to require responses to other stimuli. These, in turn, become contingencies for the presentation of the strongest reinforcement, the final step of the problem. The student, in effect, is shown how to put the last touch to the problem; as he learns each of the prior steps he finds he can continue on and complete the problem. Each time he goes on to complete a problem he has the renewed experience of receiving reinforcement for reaching a solution.

The boxed material on pages 98–99 exemplifies a learning program prepared using mathetics procedure.

The intricacies of mathetics, including its language of notation and explanation, are perhaps more than the new programmer or the teacher may wish to explore before having some personal experience with the development of a sequence. Like the analytical system of RULEG, mathetics seems to be more useful in research, in extended programming studies, and, particularly, in those instances where large blocks of subject matter are going to be handled simultaneously or in rapid succession. The method is probably more exhaustive than is required for many units that can be used immediately in the classroom. The urgencies of time and money are strong arguments for initially trying less sophisticated—but quite effective—systems of organizing program content.

OTHER APPROACHES TO SEQUENCING. Lest the beginner feel that less systematic, more pragmatic approaches to programming might not be successful in developing a sequence for item construction, there are many experts in the field who generally use an *ad hoc* process, emphasizing the value of a detailed outline

"The Color Code of Electrical Resistors," A TOR Educational Product

1. Some electrical resistors have *color bands* that tell how much they will resist electric current. On small resistors you can see colors better than numbers. Each color stands for a number.

The first three color bands are read as the number of ohms resistance.

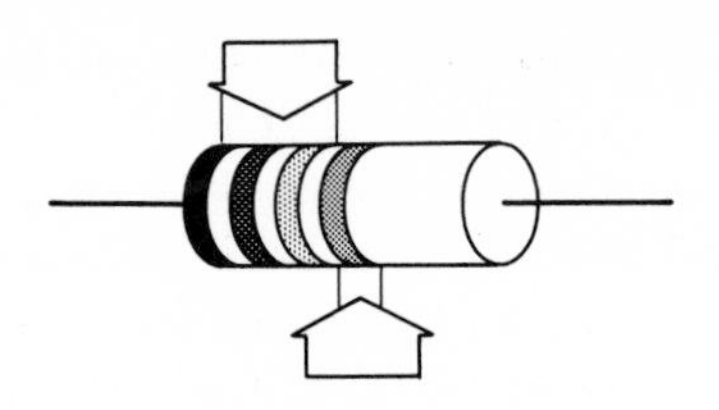

The fourth color band is read as the per cent of error in the rating.

1. *No answer required*

---

2. Resistors are not perfect and may vary a little from their rated resistance. This error is called *tolerance.* The *fourth color band* tells you how much error the manufacturer tolerated.

The color *gold* stands for 5. If a resistor's *fourth band* is *gold,* the *tolerance* will be ± _____ %.

2. 5%

D-3. If a resistor reads 250 ohms, ±10% tolerance, its true resistance may vary between 225 and 275 ohms. (± means "plus or minus.")

If a resistor reads 3600 ohms, ±10% tolerance, its true resistance may vary between __________ and __________ ohms.

If you can answer this correctly skip the next three exercises

D-3. 3240 and 3960 ohms

3A. A resistor is rated at 400 ohms, ±5% tolerance (± means "plus or minus"). To find the tolerance limits in ohms:

(a) Take 5% of 400. This equals 20.

(b) To get the lower limits of true resistance, subtract 20 from 400. This equals ____________________?

(c) To get the upper limits of true resistance, add 20 to 400. This equals ____________________?

The true resistance may vary between ____________________ and ____________________ ohms.

3A. 380 and 420 ohms

3B. A resistor is rated at 500 ohms, $\pm 20\%$ tolerance. Find the tolerance limits in ohms:
(a) Take 20% of 500.
(b) Subtract and add this value to 500.
The true resistance may vary between ________________ and ________________ ohms.

3B. 400 and 600 ohms

3C. A resistor is rated at 620 ohms, $\pm 10\%$ tolerance. The true resistance may vary between ________________ and ________________ ohms.

3C. 558 and 682 ohms

---

4. The *fourth color band* gives the *percent of error* tolerance in the resistance rating. The *fourth band* can have one of three colors; each *color* stands for a *percent*. Learn them.
Accuracy within 5% of rating—*fourth band* is *gold*
Accuracy within 10%—*fourth band* is *silver* (silver-dime)
Accuracy within 20%—*fourth band* is *black* or *missing*

4. *No answer required*

of the points to be covered in the program items. Holland, for instance, lists the following considerations in the composing of a program: [5]

1. *Specifications of a Course.* The statement of what the student is to have in his repertoire at the conclusion of the program.
2. *Knowledge Previously Acquired.* The statement of what the student is assumed to know before he starts the program.
3. *Ordering the Knowledge to Be Acquired.* A sequence of steps forming a progression from the initially assumed knowledge to the final specified repertoire. No step should be encountered by the student until he has mastered everything needed to accomplish it.
4. *Listing Terms, etc.* Before starting to write frames, the program-

[5] Holland, James G., "Programming Verbal Knowledge," Cambridge, Mass.: Harvard Psychological Laboratories, 1960, mimeo.

mer should list the terms to be covered, the processes or principles, a wide range of examples, and various item possibilities.

Holland states that "a fairly mechanical procedure can be followed in writing frames so that each concept and process will be used with each example, in as wide a range of syntactical arrangements as possible." [6]

Donald E. P. Smith has suggested these steps for the initial development and sequencing of a program.[7] He held that the programmer first should define precisely the desired behavior and the form or forms it must take. Then he should determine the steps to be learned which, when summated, will comprise the behavior. Next, he should introduce the concept, the operation, and the relationship between concept and operation, defining *all* terms to be used. Finally, he should construct a web of learning by tying the new to the old.

Another programmer, David Klaus, recommended beginning with a carefully prepared outline composed with the help of textbooks, experts, and other available aids, and then using the outline to prepare sections of the program in draft form.[8]

A similar approach has been used by George Geis who said, "It seems to be a general rule in programming that much time is spent in outlining." [9] Geis explained that he began with a broad list of concepts or topics in outline form and a second list of specific points to be included in a section. From these, he moved on to a process of outlining smaller and smaller sections in a more precise way. Then, as he started to construct program items, he reoutlined the next section of the program.

Finally, there is this view held by P. Kenneth Komoski: "Put cryptically, we submit 'that the subject matter should write the program.' As a result, we don't have a set technique." [10]

[6] *Ibid.*

[7] Smith, D. E. P., "Speculations: Characteristics of Successful Programs and Programmers" (Galanter, pp. 91–102).

[8] Klaus, David J., "Some Observations and Findings from Auto-Instructional Research," Pittsburgh, Pa.: American Institute for Research, 1960, mimeo.

[9] Geis, George L., "Program Preparation," unpublished paper, Stamford, Conn.: Public Service Research, Inc., 1961.

[10] Komoski, P. Kenneth, "Programming by Teachers for the School Curriculum," New York: Center for Programed Instruction, 1961, offset.

Each of these positions seems to reflect a concentration on the subject matter, defining in closest terms possible what the student should learn from the program, and then the pragmatic arrangement of a sequence of steps designed to take the learner from his starting point to the terminal behavior. Each of these positions would seem to presuppose that sequences will vary somewhat, and that no two programmers necessarily will arrive at identical ones. Each of them further assumes that sequencing is a dynamic process which may be changed by the experience of writing items.

A FINAL NOTE. From studying the initial efforts of classroom teachers and industrial trainers to construct programmed learning units, it becomes quite apparent that it is sufficient for them to order their items on the basis of their list of operational objectives, if these are detailed enough, or of a sequential outline designed to expand and particularize the operational objectives that they have written. More analytic measures may be desirable—although there is some coolness to them among certain programmers—but they cannot be deemed necessary.

The development of a sequence is important to initial efforts at item construction and also as a guide or check-list as the program grows. The sequence must be altered, if necessary, out of the experience gained from item writing. Very likely it will be found also to need further amplification as the program proceeds.

There may be some satisfaction in—and agreement with—these words of Geis: "No matter how carefully you outline once you start writing items you will find the previous items are a strongly controlling influence. A comparison of [a re-outline on the basis of items] and the original outlines was quite shocking. There were similarities, of course, but even my finest pre-item writing outline was different in many ways from the actual sequence I had evolved in the items." [11]

The sequence, at least for the purposes of the novice programmer, should serve as a guide, not as a brake on his developing experience.

[11] Geis, *op. cit.*

Construction of Program Items

With the preamble ended, attention may now be devoted entirely to the actual construction of program items.* Since these items, individually and in sequence, bear the brunt of the teaching design, they are the most difficult yet most rewarding part of the programming process. Let us begin by examining the elements of a typical item. Basically, an item consists of a presentation of information in appropriate context, so arranged as to require appropriate student response, with provision made for checking and instructions. Normally, the information and its arrangement repose within the stimulus portion of the item while the checking and instructions fall within the response section, as in Figure 6-2.

S. Photography comes from two Greek words:
photos meaning light
graphein meaning to write
therefore, __________ means to write with light.

R. photography *Go on to the next item*

Figure 6-2

In this case, a bit of information is given to the student: a nontechnical definition of photography. The item is so arranged that the student will respond by filling in the missing word indicated by the blank, and the construction of the item makes it quite probable that the correct, appropriate response will be made. In the response, confirmation is provided for the student who has written *photography* in the blank, and instructions are given him to go on to the next item.

* At this point, for the purpose of illustration, the discussion is limited to linear, constructed-response programming. The same technique applies to construction of intrinsic programming, examples of which may be found in Chapter 5, pp. 83–86.

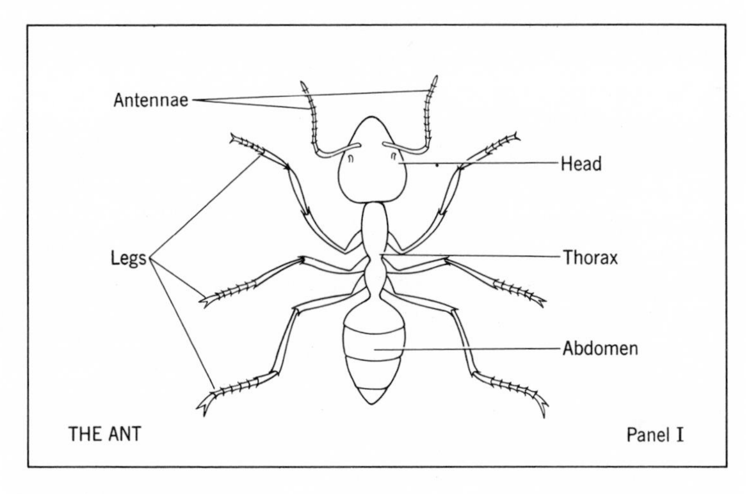

Figure 6-3

Although many items follow this basic pattern, there are times when special arrangements can be used to solve certain problems. An item may be used simply to present information without an immediate requirement for response. Quite often, however, this task will be performed by so-called *panels* of reference material, which are organized in conjunction with the program, but are handled separately by the student so that he can refer to them over a series of items. An example of such a panel—from a fifth grade program in entomology—may be observed in Figure 6-3.

How the panel is used with the program items is seen in Figure 6-4, in which the stimulus refers to the illustrated example.

S. *Examine* Panel I. Look at it as needed for items 8 through 19. We have said one of the ways to identify an insect is by its six legs. Looking at Panel I, we see the ant has ________ legs. The ant, therefore, can be identified as an ____________.

R. six or 6
insect

Figure 6-4

This item illustrates two of the more common exceptions to the general observations concerning item construction. Instructions appear in the stimulus portion of the item and are omitted in the response. Quite often, the direction "Go on to the next item" is implied unless there are instructions to the contrary.

Another special provision in the basic construction of items may occur when the programmer wishes to require student response without presenting additional material. This, of course, might be done for review, or to serve as a terminal item for a sequence to check whether the student actually has mastered the lesson to this point. A typical item might look like S-13 in Figure 6-5; for the sake of continuity, a portion of the preceding sequence is included.

Still another exception to the general construction rule arises when the programmer desires to provide instructions to the learner without either presenting new information or arranging for a response to previous information. Such an item might read as in Figure 6-6.

S-6. There are a number of assumptions we (the programmers) must make about you (the learner). One is that you read at a certain level and have a vocabulary consistent with this program. Programmers must make __________ about the learner.

R-6. assumptions

S-8. We, as programmers, not only have to make certain assumptions about you, the learner, but we also must determine the goals or *objectives* of the program. The goals or __________ as well as the *assumptions* are integral parts of programming for automated instruction

R-8. objectives

S-13. Two important considerations of "programmed learning" are to make (a) __________ about the learner and to determine the (b) __________ of the program.

R-13. (a) assumptions
(b) objectives

Figure 6-5

S-42. Review your response sheet for items 15 through 41. If you have two or more errors go on to item 43. If you have less than two errors, go on to item 50.

Figure 6-6

One final exception has been described by Lewis Eigen as a *forcing* item since it gives no obvious information to the student, but does force him to respond correctly even though there may be no essentially rational basis for his response.[12] Such items, as seen in Figure 6-7, can be used to introduce new sequences or operations.

S-82. The last two parts of speech to be considered are the gerund and the participle. First, we will look at the gerund; then, the ________.

R-82. participle

Figure 6-7

A typical item in an extrinsic program, then, has three components: a presentation of information in appropriate context, arranged to require a correct response, with provision made for checks and instructions. From time to time, programmers may care to use only one of these components without incorporating the other two in the same item. That is, they may wish to provide content information or data for the student to observe without requiring an immediate response; or they may, in order to review or check mastery, require a response to an item which is devoid of information; or they may simply use a frame to provide instructions or directions to the student.

THE INFORMATION COMPONENT. One basic element of item construction, as has been noted, is to present information to the student in appropriate context. Let us examine various ways

[12] Eigen, Lewis, "The Construction of Frames of an Automated Teaching Program," New York: Center for Programed Instruction, 1960, offset.

S. A line that runs straight up and down is called a vertical line. The line at the side of this item is a vertical line. A flagpole would be an example of a __________ line.

R. vertical

S. To explain motivated behavior, we need to look at three things:

Need → Behavior → Goal

In order to satisfy a certain need, a person __________ in a certain way to achieve some goal which he feels will fill this need.

R. behaves

Figure 6-8

of handling this component so that student learning will be facilitated. While programming essentially is a dynamic and unfolding art, the approaches proposed here have been found by many beginners to be helpful in their efforts. First, the use of examples and simple definitions in introducing new concepts, as in Figures 6-8 and 6-9.

S. The number of people in a family may also cause expense to vary. A family of two will often have less food __________ than a family of five.

R. expense

S. People began to count long before they had numbers. By notching a stick, knotting a cord, putting pebbles in a bowl, they kept track of the passing of sheep or the measures of grain. In time, these tedious means of enumerating were replaced with written symbols called numbers.

Written __________ called numbers replaced the old and tedious methods of counting.

R. symbols

Figure 6-9

Second, the use of appropriate context including graphic illustrations to develop understanding of the information content, as in Figures 6-10, 6-11, and 6-12.

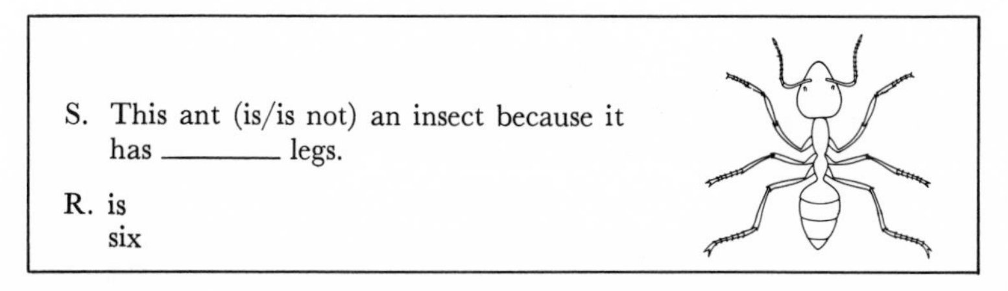

Figure 6-10

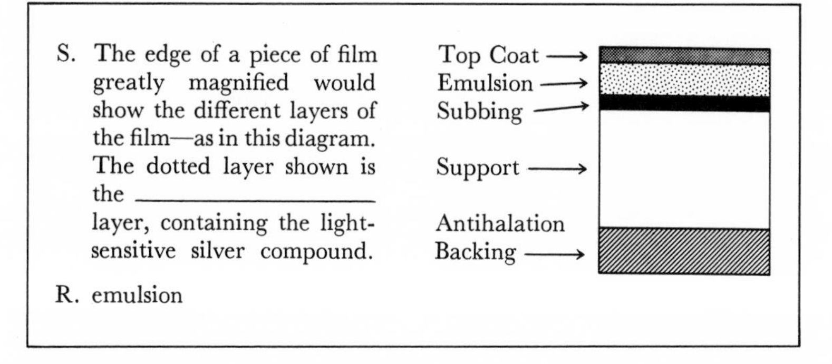

Figure 6-11

S. Some of the fascinating properties have come down to us in such forms as the "magic" number squares, one of which is shown below:

16	3	2	13
5	10	11	8
9	6	7	12
4	15	14	1

The sum of the numbers in any column, row, or diagonal is the same. The sum of the numbers in the first column is ________.

R. 34

Figure 6-12

Third, the use of small steps with careful sequencing, as in Figure 6-13.

S. *Quad* means four. *Lateral* refers to side. A *quadrilateral* always has four sides. A square would be one type of quadrilateral. The figures below are all __________ because they have four sides.

R. quadrilaterals

S. A rectangle is a quadrilateral because it always has __________ sides.

R. four

S. A rectangle is one type of __________ because it has __________ sides.

R. quadrilateral
four

S. A square is a type of __________ because it has __________ sides.

R. quadrilateral
four

S. All figures that have four sides are known as __________ .

R. quadrilaterals

Figure 6-13

S. In Pavlov's experiment, the ticking of the metronome elicited salivation. The conditioned stimulus was the ______.

R. ticking

S. In the Pavlov experiment, the ticking of the metronome was the ______.

R. conditioned stimulus

S. The conditioned stimulus, the ticking of a metronome, elicited salivation. Salivation, then, is described as a conditioned ______.

R. response

S. Salivation at the ticking of a metronome is an example of a (an) ______.

R. conditioned response

Figure 6-14

Fourth, the use of frequent but varied repetition, as may be seen in Figure 6-14.

The foregoing illustrations suggest the many ways in which the programmer can fashion the information content of a program item to facilitate the learning of the material by the student. Brevity, use of examples, appropriate context, and graphic illustrations all provide significant help to the learner. Similarly, small steps, careful sequencing, and frequent repetition give the student an opportunity to develop a better conceptual picture of the unfolding program.

ARRANGING FOR STUDENT RESPONSE. Just as with the information component of a program item, the programmer must arrange for appropriate student response, generally striving to forestall student error. There are a number of techniques which the beginner at programming can draw upon in arranging for student response. Several examples undoubtedly will suggest many more possibilities to the reader.

The programmer must make certain the required response is relevant, as demonstrated in Figure 6-15. He must use mechanical devices to focus the student's attention and to assist him to respond correctly; this includes underlining, bold face type, italicizing, color keying, and similar techniques, as shown by Figures 6-16 and 6-17. He should use text, grammatical con-

S. You should complete each item in this program by writing your constructed ______________ on the response sheet.

NOT THIS

S. You ______________ ______________ each item in this program by writing your constructed response on the response sheet.

Figure 6-15

S. All meetings, lectures, or training programs attended by employees *during regular working hours* are ______________ as time worked.

R. considered or paid for

Figure 6-16

S. Most families' *income* consists of earnings of the employed members of the family. Some of the family earnings or ______________ must be expended for such things as food, clothing, and shelter.

R. income

Figure 6-17

S. A *proper* noun names a *particular* person, place or thing. John, Austria, Rochester, Genesee River are all proper nouns. New York is a ______________ noun because it is the name of a ______________ state.

R. proper
particular

S. River is *not* a ______________ noun because it is not the name of a particular person, place or thing. Hudson River is a ______________ noun.

R. proper
proper

Figure 6-18

S. We reward a dog after it has performed a trick; therefore, reward or reinforcement should ______________ a response.

R. follow

Figure 6-19

S. When the voltage is held constant, an increase in resistance results in a decrease in current; naturally, then, a decrease in resistance leads to an ______________ in current.

R. increase

Figure 6-20

struction, or both, to aid the student in understanding new concepts or material, as in Figures 6-18 through 6-23. He should use common knowledge or words with high association value to aid in developing correct student response, as in Figures 6-24 through 6-26. He should use fading or vanishing to reduce the number of cues gradually and make the student response independent of assistance, as may be observed in Figure 6-27.

While these techniques will assist the learner in arriving at the correct response, it should be kept in mind that they represent, to some degree, a touch of artificiality. To the extent that the programmer can use the *implicit logic* of his subject

> S. The hotter the filament, the brighter the lamp. The cooler the filament, the less ______________ the lamp.
>
> R. bright

Figure 6-21

> S. Vowels are a, e, o, u and i, and, sometimes, also the letter ______.
>
> R. y

Figure 6-22

> S. The + sign stands for addition; the ÷ sign stands for d________n.
>
> R. division

Figure 6-23

> S. A thirsty animal can be reinforced or rewarded with ________.
>
> R. water

Figure 6-24

S. When we toss a coin in the air the probability of its coming up heads is ________ chance out of two.

R. one

Figure 6-25

S. A puff of air strikes you in the eye. If your reflexes are normal, your eye will ______________ to the puff of air by blinking or winking.

R. respond or react

Figure 6-26

S. The word PREDICT comes from two Latin words

pre meaning *before*

and

dicto meaning *to tell*

Predict, then, means to tell beforehand. Copy the word here ______

S. Part of the word predict comes from an old word meaning to tell or speak.

pre______ (complete spelling the word)

S. A modern English word meaning to tell beforehand is:

____

S. If we forecast an event before it happens, we would ________ it.

Figure 6-27

matter in preparing his program—that is, by proper ordering, sufficient repetition, and sufficient preparation and introductory materials—he can relate it to real life and avoid to a greater degree the necessity for cues and promptings.

CHECKING AND INSTRUCTION. The third basic element in most program items is that which provides information to the student as to the correctness and adequacy of his response, and, in some cases, additional information and instruction. These portions of the item usually are dictated by the construction of the first two components of the item, but they permit the programmer additional control over the learning behavior of the student. Some considerations regarding the use of checks and instruction include the confirmation of the response of the student and indicate alternatives and synonyms if they are admissible, as in Figure 6-28. They also include use of confirmation of the item to supply additional information to the student, as shown by Figure 6-29. In addition, they use the confirmation to provide instructions on student use of the program, as seen in Figure 6-30.

S. In other words, the federal rules state the condition under which training outside regular working hours need not be ____________ as time worked.

R. *considered* or *paid for* or *calculated* or another reasonable term.

S. Technically speaking, a thirsty animal can be ____________ with water.

R. reinforced
Note: not reward, you were asked to speak *technically*.

S. $40.5 \div 3.6 =$ ________.

R. 11.222
Note: Did you carry your answer to three places?

Figure 6-28

S. One explanation that has been advanced for behavior is that of innate or instinctive drives. Instinct, then, is regarded by some people as an explanation for ______________.

R. behavior
Note: Innate comes from Latin words meaning *inborn*. We shall use it often as we consider the matter of instinct.

S. $\frac{1}{4} + \frac{5}{8} + \frac{7}{12} + \frac{2}{3} =$ __________.

R. $2\frac{1}{8}$
Note: If your response is not the same, did you use 24 as a common denominator, and did you reduce your answer to a mixed fraction?

Figure 6-29

S. The two special conditions of the federal rules which apply to apprentices are:
(a) ________________________
(b) ________________________

R. (a) attendance may be required
(b) attendance need not be compensated
Note: If you could not state these conditions—or if you are not certain of their interpretation—return to item 41 and re-read the program material.

S. The next consideration is that of the mean. If six students scored the following on a test, 70, 95, 75, 100, 80, and 85, what would be the mean grade?

R. 84.2
Note: If your response is incorrect—or if you have no idea about solving for the mean—go on to the next item. If your response is correct, you may go on to item 14.

Figure 6-30

OTHER CONSIDERATIONS. In addition to the development of the basic components of program items, it might be well to think in terms of specific uses of particular items in the unfolding learning experience. Certain of these uses are review, generalization, specification, interlocking, and termination.

Several times in the treatment of programs and program writing, the need for built-in review has been emphasized. In the process of writing items, however, the value of three kinds of review material should be appreciated. The first is simply *rote* or *repetitive* material which appears in items immediately following the initial development. A second type of review item utilizes *restatement in a slightly different context* as a method of ascertaining that the student has some mobility in absorbing the information he has learned. The third type of review is *delayed repetition* which occasionally is injected into the program sequence to check that understanding is being retained and carried along throughout the program.

A generalization item presents a general statement or rule to provide a common characteristic for specific material covered in previous items. For instance, an item in a mathematics program might develop this sort of generalization: "We have seen that one perpendicular is needed to divide a line into two equal parts; likewise two perpendiculars are needed to divide a line into three equal parts. Therefore, we could extend this idea by stating that if n equals the number of equal parts we desire, then we need ________ perpendiculars."

Specification items are used to determine a student's ability to apply general rules already learned to particular situations or conditions. "An employee, John Doe, is registered in a degree program at the University of Rochester. According to the federal rules we have discussed, he (would/would not) be entitled to compensation for his time spent in class."

Interlocking items are used to link new material to that already learned, and to function as a bridge to further development of the new content. "We have considered the case of a dog salivating at the sight of meat. We call this an ________ response. We will now look at the same behavior, salivating, but as a conditioned response."

Terminating items are used to conclude developmental sequences in a program so that the student can demonstrate his understanding and mastery. Typically, all cues have vanished before the terminal item, which might appear simply like this: "Name the four steps in the photographic process: (a) ________, (b) ________, (c) ________, (d) ________."

No emphasis on the writing of individual items should end without stressing the importance of considering them as individual components or ingredients of a coaching system to develop mastery of learning. At all times, they must be viewed in integrated form, as leading the learner from known to unknown, from simple to complex, from concrete to abstract. The true measure of any item is the extent to which it aids the student in following the route laid out by the programmer.

While the suggestions made in this chapter for writing items have evolved from experience, there is no adequate judge of an item's value short of the student for whom the item is intended. In the final analysis, the student will write, or re-write, the items for the programmer—and therefore the sequences and the program—on the basis of his own responses.

SELECTED READINGS

1. Eigen, Lewis D., "The Construction of Frames of an Automated Teaching Program," revised edition, New York: Center for Programed Instruction, 1960, mimeo.

This paper represents one of the first attempts to describe the writing of program items.

2. Galanter, Eugene (Ed.), *Automatic Teaching: The State of the Art,* New York: John Wiley and Sons, 1959.

Smith, Donald E. P., "Speculations: Characteristics of Successful Programs and Programmers," pp. 91–102.

A concise statement of considerations in programming material for auto-instruction.

3. Gilbert, Thomas F., "An Early Approximation of Principles of Analyzing and Revising Self-Instructional Programs," unpublished paper, December, 1958.

Although this paper is unpublished, it is cited because the Lumsdaine and Glaser source book provides an extensive précis of Gilbert's work on pages 629–634. The same editors cite a limited publication of the article as part of a report for the United States Office of Education. This report may be available to some readers. See Lumsdaine and Glaser, page 636.

4. Lumsdaine, Arthur A., and Robert Glaser (Eds.), *Teaching Machines and Programmed Learning: A Source Book,* Washington, D.C.: NEA, 1960.

Holland, James G., "Teaching Machines: An Application of Principles from the Laboratory," pp. 215–228.

Homme, Lloyd E., and Robert Glaser, "Problems in Programming Verbal Learning Sequences," pp. 486–496.

Skinner, B. F., "Teaching Machines," pp. 137–158.

Skinner, B. F., and James G. Holland, "The Use of Teaching Machines in College Instruction," pp. 159–172.

These and other articles in the source book are helpful in understanding item construction. The paper by Homme and Glaser explains the RULEG approach in some detail.

5. Margulies, Stuart, and Lewis D. Eigen (Eds.), *Applied Programed Instruction,* New York: John Wiley and Sons, 1962.

Pennington, D. F., and C. W. Slack, "The Mathetical Design of Effective Lessons," pp. 298–310.

This is a brief explanation of the programming approach known as "mathetics."

6. Weaver, David O., "Suggested Techniques in Preparing Programmed Learning," *Journ. of Am. Soc. of Training Dirs.,* May, 1961.

An article of interest to industrial training specialists.

Chapter Seven

Editing and Review

Programming is pragmatic in nature, an expert in the field has commented. What works is kept, what fails is rejected. Therefore, any novel approach may prove astonishingly valuable when preparing material for self-instruction.[1] For this reason, it behooves the programmer to test the items of his learning sequence with his students as soon as possible. He may discover that he has hit upon a fruitful new idea or has struck out ingloriously. At times, it is convenient to try the items immediately after they have been written. In other instances, especially when expert assistance is available to the programmer, it is beneficial to have the material edited before it is tested with the students.

When the latter circumstance prevails, a natural procedure for handling the programmed items presents itself. First, the items are edited. Next, they are subjected to immediate field tests. Then they are reviewed and rewritten. The editing in this sense is of a limited kind; it is not akin to editing material for publication, as shall become evident presently. Similarly, the terms *review* and *rewrite* are used in preference to *revision* to indicate that some changes probably will have to be made after a brief field test, but that the larger task of complete revision had better wait upon more extensive practice with the program.

[1] Eigen, Lewis D., "The Construction of Frames of an Automated Teaching Program," revised, New York: Center for Programed Instruction, 1960, mimeo.

Editing the Items

The programmer may choose, of course, to precede any editorial work on his items with a field test of them, and this is a perfectly valid procedure. But when special consultants are handy, a check of the program from two standpoints prior to exposing it to students invariably serves a worthwhile purpose. The two factors of editorial significance are the accuracy and relevance of the material, and the style and vocabulary of the unit and interest of its content.

ACCURACY AND RELEVANCE OF MATERIAL. In this respect, the help of a subject-matter specialist—and preferably one who is also an excellent teacher—is of great advantage. The programmer and his consultant should read the sequence without looking too closely at individual items for a general impression of the work. Then they should ask themselves the following kinds of questions: Does this sequence generally cover the material specified in the objectives of the program? Does it represent a real learning guide? That is, does it provide the student with a reasonably developed conceptual understanding of the subject matter? Or does it merely give some disparate information? Is the context of the material useful and appropriate to the subject matter? Are the examples well chosen and meaningful? Generally, does the sequence seem to be in agreement with the assumptions about the learners for whom it is intended? Has more or less been assumed in the program than was intended to be assumed?

After these general questions have been answered, a more detailed re-reading of the sequence, item by item, may be undertaken. Once this has been completed, the programmer and the specialist should amend the material, if necessary, in the light of the aforementioned points and these: Are the responses required of the student really relevant and important to the subject matter? In fact, do the responses include all the important subject matter of the sequence? What is the relation between stimuli and responses? Do the responses follow logically and without ambiguity from the stimuli? Is each stimulus presenting its information correctly? Is each response used correctly throughout the program sequence? Has anything of importance to the objectives been omitted in the sequence? Has extraneous or undesirable information been included?

Following this phase of editing, any substantive errors or omissions should be clarified, and the programmer should be fairly confident that his material is correct and reasonably ordered.

STYLE, VOCABULARY, AND CONTENT INTEREST. As the programmer uses the criticism of the subject-matter specialist, so will he find it productive to have the assistance of a person with writing experience—especially experience in writing for students at the level appropriate to the program. As before, it is desirable to read the program over twice, once for an over-all impression of vocabulary and style, the second time for the writing of particular items.

This aspect of the editing should direct itself to questions about construction of the items, such as: Is the reading level of the program in line with the assumptions about the learner? Is it too difficult? Or does it talk down to the students? Does it enrich the vocabulary of the students? Are new words defined as they are introduced? Is there variety in the style and sequencing of the program? Would a student find it interesting and exciting, or dull and extremely repetitious? Are the review items handled entirely by rote? Or are new examples and restatement employed? Are certain responses or stimulus-response combinations used so frequently that responding ceases to be active and students might tend to be bored? Is sufficient use made of graphic illustration? Would pictures, drawings, graphs, or charts add to the understanding and interest of items? Is there variation in the positioning of the response sections, in length or type, to insure that undesirable learning *sets* are not induced?

If editing does precede immediate field testing of the program, it may help to prevent errors of both content and style. Nevertheless, this form of editing only approximates the behavior of the student with regard to the program, and no programmer should think, once it is finished, that the program is firmly settled.

Immediate Field Testing

For initial field testing of the program, the programmer requires only a sample number of students who fit his assumptions. There is some advantage to having thirty to thirty-five students involved in the program, and most teachers will find this number in their own classrooms. On the other hand, effective field testing has been done with even fewer students, particularly by industrial training specialists who have a smaller number of students at their disposal for trying out an experimental program.

Students should be given the appropriate instructions for working with the program, and should begin to labor at it. In completing the customary response sheets, they should be encouraged to write comments or questions after each response as to whether they regard the item as confusing, difficult, repetitious, or particularly helpful. Also, they should record the times started and completed.

Equally important for the programmer is information about student reaction. This can be obtained partially from the response sheets or tapes, but better from sitting down with a few students and observing them as they go through the material. In addition to watching responses, the programmer can spot hesitation, evidence of confusion or frustration, and the effect of the program on student motivation. He even may wish to note time spent on particular items.

When students have completed the program, they should be questioned immediately about their reactions and the subject matter in order to obtain a general approximation of the program's effectiveness. Many programmers have found a brief, post-test inquiry truly helpful in pointing out how well the students have learned. They have taken pains, incidentally, in numerous cases to give the students strong assurance that the test has nothing to do with their grade in the course, and that the experience is not a regular part of the instruction.

It is important to collate the results recorded on the response sheets and also the gleanings of the post-test inquiry when this is administered during the field test. Errors should be itemized; time should be recorded, both for total time consumed and for particular items, if the teacher finds in individual student cases that some portions of the program demand an inordinate amount of time and effort.

All this material is the raw stuff for reviewing and rewriting the program prior to larger scale trial and revision. It should be studied carefully to see if the students actually seem to learn from the sequence as it stands, and also to see what improvements can be made in the items, or groups of items, to enhance the learning experience.

Perhaps something should be said about the mechanical aspects of the immediate field test. Many newcomers to programming write their initial items on small index cards. This facilitates correction and permits simplicity in changing the order of particular items by a shifting of the cards. For the field test, additional sets of cards or sheets containing four to six items each are supplied. The emphasis, of course, is on some inexpensive means of preparing the program for testing since the probability of its requiring changes is high. Only after extensive experience with students, and after several revisions, will the program be likely to be ready for more permanent reproduction.

Likewise, the response sheet for student use in field testing should be simple and inexpensive. One of the most satisfactory is a sheet of 8½ x 11 paper arranged so that a vertical line divides it into two columns. In the lefthand column, students construct their responses. In the righthand column, they correct their responses, if necessary, and write any questions or comments they have about the stimulus or the response. This form simplifies the collection of information from the students and permits rapid inspection of troublesome items. A portion of such a form appears in Figure 7-1.

With the completion of the field test, and the collection of information contained on the student response sheets, the programmer is ready to move on to the review and rewriting of those items shown to be weak or defective.

Science — Grade 5 — Name ______ — Date ______

Response Sheet

Responses	Corrected Responses and Comments
Set A.	
Record the time ______	
A-1 ______	______
A-2 ______	______
A-3 ______	______
A-4 ______	______
A-5 ______	______
A-50 ______	______
	Record your finishing time ______

Figure 7-1

Reviewing and Rewriting Items

From the evidence of student performance, the programmer can examine each item of his sequence with a view toward analyzing its effectiveness and attempting to improve it. There are several specific pitfalls for which he should be searching.

ERRORS AND ERROR LEVEL. Incorrect responses by students to particular items should be studied in an attempt to analyze their causes. The incorrect response recorded by the student often will provide the best clue to the source of the error. The student response, for instance, usually will indicate whether the mistake was substantive or procedural, whether the student misunderstood the stimulus, or simply made a mistake in calculation or spelling.

The different nature of the mistakes provides a means for preventing their recurrence. Substantive errors may require the rewriting of particular items, as well as an examination of the items that constitute the development leading to those items. Procedural mistakes may require the use of more review items to give students an additional opportunity to practice their handling of material and problems.

Error level refers to the percentage of students who make errors on a given frame. As a rule of thumb, many programmers ignore errors that fall below the 5 per cent level—that is, items that at least 95 per cent of the students answer correctly. Actually, the numerical element is best kept elastic as the programmer may believe that certain items may exceed the 5 per cent level without endangering the understanding of the sequence, whereas he may be concerned over *any* errors recorded on terminal items. Whichever the case, item analysis of errors plays a positive role in focusing attention on outstanding weaknesses in the internal structure of the program.

LENGTH OF ITEMS. When errors point to problems in a specific item, one of the possible causes to be explored is that of the item's length. Actually, this involves two considerations. One of the principal reasons for student error on items—or on subsequent items—is the tendency to make steps in the program too wordy; or the programmer may begin to lecture rather than to program. The item resembles a discourse more than a stimulus, and the student is confused by the amount of material and its lack of direction. Extraneous facts can make for easy misunderstanding.

In addition to the sheer matter of length, there is the problem, even in a relatively short item, of teaching more than one element at a time. In a sense, this refers to the density rather than the length of the item. Either way, items that try to cover too much ground are responsible for a large percentage of student errors.

LEVEL OF DIFFICULTY. A clustering of incorrect responses indicates that an item may be constructed at too high a level of difficulty for the student to master. One should examine the recorded responses closely, and ask: Is there too large a step—or conceptual leap—from the preceding item to this item? Does the item follow logically and understandably? Is there any particular difficulty in vocabulary or technical terminology that was not anticipated by previous items?

Another consideration with regard to the difficulty of an item is the error rate of previous items. They should be examined in sequence to determine whether the error is a growing accumulation of misunderstanding, or is attributable only to the item in question.

AMBIGUITY AND CONFUSION. Another cause for student error is lack of clarity in the item. This, also, often will be indicated by the record of student responses. Lack of constructed responses on some items, or a response which is quite different from the one expected, is an indication that the item is confusing or ambiguous. In such cases, a programmer might inquire: Are too many responses called for in an item? Are there so many blanks that the item loses its understandability and logical development? Is there confusion as to what response the student is expected to make? Is the item logically or semantically incomplete? Is the required response relevant? Or is the student error the result of an item requiring an irrelevant or insignificant response? Has the item assumed that the response can be generated from the student's background knowledge—without previous groundwork being laid?

As in the cases of other kinds of problems, ambiguous items usually can be cleared up by inserting additional items into the sequence, and by rewriting existing items to make certain that the response is both relevant and logically derived from the stimulus.

CUEING AND FADING. Incorrect responses at the early stage of a program sequence may be indicative of a lack of cueing and prompting to focus student attention effectively on the important parts of the subject matter. On the other hand, too much prompting can result in a student never making an error on an item, but never mastering the material, either. The programmer should examine the record of student responses for evidence of both kinds of problems. He should refer also to the results of his post-test check or should arrange to discuss the program with the students after the field test in order to ascertain whether they have learned effectively. Certainly, the programmer should examine the items with these questions in mind: Is the cueing and prompting adequate? Are errors attributable to a lack of student recognition of important elements? Particularly on items introducing new material or new terms is the cueing strong enough to control student response behavior? Is the cueing gradually reduced so that the terminal frames of a sequence are responded to by the student out of his acquired knowledge without benefits of prompts? Is the cueing so heavy that it conflicts with active responding by supplying too much help to the student? Do the cues simply encourage rote handling of the material? Are cueing and prompting handled in a variety of ways to avoid the program's developing a "system" to which the student can respond rather than study the items as they appear?

One danger to be avoided in reviewing and rewriting frames is to reduce errors simply by inserting more cues into the items. This, of course, will mean fewer errors. The post-test, however, might show that unfortunately no learning took place because no learning procedure had been developed.

Further Considerations in Reviewing Items

So much for the errors committed by students as the result of item length, difficulty, ambiguity, or cueing. Another concern in reviewing student response and reaction to the field testing pertains to the effectiveness of the program in the areas of learning development and motivation.

Are students accomplishing the objectives? In examining the positive effects of the program, the programmer should study the responses and reactions to see whether the program actually is achieving the learning objectives to which it was addressed. If a post-test inquiry has not been used to assist in this portion of the review, the programmer will want to discuss the material with the students to ascertain the hold their learning has taken, and to assess the conceptual depth of their knowledge. Do the students demonstrate growth, the programmer might ask himself, by their ability to discuss and apply concepts and by their correct use of the technical vocabulary in the program? Do they display confidence in their over-all grasp of the material, or do they seem to have only an understanding of certain discrete learnings without a general frame of reference? Do they think they have had sufficient review material and practice items to assure their grasp of the program? Do they demonstrate an ability to transfer the learnings of the program and apply them to situations not covered by it?

Many of these points, of course, are best indicated by the behavior of the student in class discussion or in work assignments based on the program content. The programmer should endeavor to discover, therefore, how the student may handle the material outside the confines of the programmed sequence.

Are students satisfied? One result to be sought from use of the program is an increase in the positive feeling or attitude of the student toward the subject matter based on the effects of reinforcement and success in learning. Did students find the program interesting and challenging? Did they consider the content varied and the examples interesting and helpful? Were they interested in pursuing the program and in finding out more about the subject matter? Did they believe that the program was too difficult or too easy? Did they find the content boring or redundant? A successful program should promote strong, favorable attitudes or feelings toward subject matter, and the programmer should single out any negative reactions in order to eliminate their cause.

Examples of Defective Items

Defective items indicate some of the more common errors made by inexperienced programmers. It is impossible, of course, to display all the problems to be encountered. A sample of them is enough to underscore the facts that student error is a reflection of an error in programming, and that a multiplicity of errors is cause for concern and corrective action. The examples and comments on typical defective items shown in Figures 7-2, 7-3, and 7-4 may be of help in avoiding pitfalls.

S-1. The sun is the center of the ________ ________.

R-1. solar system

(This introductory item is constructed like a test item. There is no introduction of terms or understandings. The student might respond correctly, but the entire burden of the item is on the learner and most probably the response will be incorrect or incomplete.)

S-1. If there is evidence of misconduct in office by a president or a federal judge, the House of Representatives can accuse or ________ him.

R-1. impeach

(This item does present more information for the student to use in framing his response, but the term *impeach* has not been developed, and the student might well use an improper term—or even respond quite incorrectly by inferring a term like *imprison* or *try* in place of the desired one. The item could lead to very faulty learning.)

Figure 7-2

Continued Review and Rewriting

As the weaknesses and faults of a program are exposed in the initial testing, they are reviewed and corrected by the programmer. Usually, if the program has been developed in an orderly process of selection, stated assumptions, specified objectives, and careful construction, the field test will show up the areas that need improvement, but is not likely to uncover any problems of a critical nature.

When the programmer has completed the rewriting of the items, he can proceed to further trial use of the program as a preliminary to a larger revision, if that seems indicated by the student responses. The succeeding chapter shall explore the more detailed evaluation of a program that has been field tested. Revision generally can be accomplished on the basis of such an evaluation.

In many cases, the classroom teacher or the industrial training specialist may choose to go no further than the evaluation stage

S-1. You have some 206 bones making up your skeleton. At first, the skeleton is made up of a soft substance called cartilage. Later, the bone cells begin to develop. First, the skeleton is made up of a soft substance called ______________.

R-1. cartilage

(Although most students would respond correctly to this item, this is an example of a stimulus which actually assumes the proportion of a lecture rather than an item. In one swoop, the student is given the number of bones in the skeleton, some information about cartilage, and the knowledge that there are "bone cells" that develop. A more gradual development of this material over several items, properly sequenced, would be an improvement.)

S-1. If you do not find the information as quickly as you had anticipated, return __________ __________, use an ______ ______ explain that __________, and ask if the caller still wishes to wait.

(In this case, without considering the responses, we can see that the item contains many problems of vagueness and ambiguity for the learner. Too much is asked for, and the result is very likely to be inadequate, incorrect, or both.)

S-1. Air passes from the nose or mouth down the windpipe or trachea to the two bronchial tubes. Each bronchial tube branches to form smaller tubes. These small tubes go to many air sacs or alvioli of the lungs. The exchange of oxygen and carbon dioxide occurs in the ______________.

(This item contains too much material and nowhere does it guide the student to an understanding that would result in an appropriate response. Also, this item illustrates the need for an explanatory panel or figure to aid the student in learning the parts of the body being discussed.)

S-1. When you as a secretary answer your office telephone, you speak ______________.

(This item provides almost no control over the student response. The replies might range from "for the company" to "for forty-five minutes." This type of item invites confusion and student dismay. There are times for the student to compose his response in his own words, but only after he has developed understanding and a grasp of the material.)

Figure 7-3

S-30. Nine planets and the planetoids travel in nearly circular orbits around the center of the solar system. The center of the solar system is called the ______________.

(This item actually was intended to be a terminal frame for a sequence on the solar system. The programmer, however, has summarized the sequence for the learner, and the only response required of the student is to that portion of the material that was covered early in the sequence. As a terminal frame, this requires too little of the student, and, moreover, could be criticized for using cues even at this stage of the program for an understanding that supposedly was learned much earlier.)

S-1. The President, sometimes called the ______________ ______________, is at the head of the Executive Branch.

(In this case, the item calls for student response based on information acquired outside the material. More importantly, however, the response called for is relatively unimportant to the sense of the item itself. The response should be particularly relevant to the sense and scheme of the item.)

S-32. If a bill is ______________ by the President, the bill doesn't become a law unless it goes back to Congress and is approved by a *two-thirds* majority in both houses. By the use of the veto, the President has a check on the Legislative Branch. Rarely can Congress get enough votes to pass a bill over a presidential veto.

(Here, the programmer is lecturing, and goes well beyond the area indicated by the nature of the response. In cases such as this, the student could respond correctly to the first portion of the item, and never read the remainder. The length of the item, and the quantity of material contained in it should be distributed over several items.)

S-2. Write in what you think each of these symbols mean, and then turn the page to see if you have done it correctly.

S^2 S SA A A^2

(Again, this is a test item rather than a program item. It has the real danger of causing frustration, or, just as likely, of developing an incorrect response on the part of the student that will have to be extinguished before he can learn the proper definition of the terms.)

Figure 7-4

of the program. There simply may be a desire to gain experience with the technique and to forego a number of revisions that might be desirable from the commercial programmer's point of view. As a matter of fact, if the programmer is working on a fairly short unit of material, his evaluation may well indicate that extensive revision is unnecessary, and that the corrective action taken after the first field test is entirely adequate. This is a distinct possibility when the teacher or trainer is working with a group of students which compares closely with his assumptions about the learners.

By now, the programmer will understand why the construction of items is likely to be the most demanding and the most satisfying part of the programming process. Only one more step remains—evaluation.

SELECTED READINGS

1. Galanter, Eugene (Ed.), *Automatic Teaching: The State of the Art,* New York: John Wiley and Sons, 1959.

Holland, James G., "A Teaching Machine Program in Psychology," pp. 69–82.

This article specifies a number of items from the Holland-Skinner program in psychology together with an analysis of errors on those items.

2. Klaus, David J., "The Art of Auto-Instructional Programming," A.I.R. Memorandum No. 15, Pittsburgh, Pa.: American Institute for Research, 1960, offset.

This small booklet will be of interest to any beginning programmer. Klaus makes excellent use of examples to illustrate both good and poor program items. He also points out ways to improve those items that are less than effective.

3. Lumsdaine, Arthur A., and Robert Glaser (Eds.), *Teaching Machines and Programmed Learning: A Source Book,* Washington, D.C.: NEA, 1960.

Amsel, Abram, "Error Responses and Reinforcement Schedules in Self-Instructional Devices," pp. 506–516.

Lumsdaine, Arthur A., "Some Issues Concerning Devices and Programs for Automated Learning," pp. 517–539.

Meyer, Susan R., "Report on the Initial Test of a Junior High-School Vocabulary Program," pp. 229–246.

These papers represent variant approaches to the matter of student error. Amsel suggests that minimizing errors may not be desirable in all learning situations. Lumsdaine considers some of the factors (such as size-of-step) which affect errors. Meyer reports an analysis of student performance and errors on a program.

4. *Newer Educational Media,* papers of the Regional Research Conference, University Park, Pa.: Pennsylvania State University, in cooperation with the U.S. Department of Health, Education, and Welfare, 1961.

Glaser, Robert, "Principles and Problems in the Preparation of Programmed Learning Sequences," pp. 19–42.

An overview of the writing and revision of programmed material.

5. *Programed Instruction,* Center for Programed Instruction, New York.

This newsletter, published on a quarterly basis, has a regular feature entitled "Faulty Frames." In this section, an ineffective sequence is analyzed and revised to produce desired student behavior.

Chapter Eight

Evaluation

Now and then a school or business firm will report to the educational fraternity that it is testing a program on some specific piece of learning. If asked to describe the tests the program is undergoing, those in charge express bewilderment. They explain that no tests are being applied, but that the program itself is under scrutiny. From further discussion it becomes apparent that some confusion exists, not only about the distinctions between programs and tests, but also about the nomenclature of measurement.

Testing, in relation to the programming of auto-instructional materials, refers to the administration of a test, a device designed to elicit information about the particular responses that are made to particular stimuli. A score or a set of scores, for example, might be obtained through testing at the scene and then compared with national averages. Thus, the similarities and differences in the way the local group reacts to the test can be noted and defined in comparison to the performance of a much larger, nationwide body of students.

Evaluation, on the other hand, is a more inclusive term. It denotes the making of judgments or decisions based on the assemblage and analysis of diverse types of data. These may be gathered from objective tests, observations, anecdotal records, and many other sources, and used singly or in various combinations as factors to be weighed in rendering evaluations. In a broad sense, evaluation also extends to the testing activities in which a programmer engages when he tries out his program on a small number of learners as part of the complete programming process.

The Programmer's Problems

As noted in the previous chapter, the programmer should submit his sequence to a few of the learners who conform to his assumptions as soon as he has completed a few items. The resulting data will assist him to discover items that are confusing, difficult, repetitious, or, in contrast, particularly helpful. It will also tell him things about the time needed to complete the sequence and the reactions of the learners. In addition to guiding the programmer to editing and further writing, this preliminary information constitutes a primary data pool about the program. Should the programmer learn that his first twenty items take about 30 minutes, on the average, to complete and that there is little variance from the average, he can extrapolate tentatively that his entire program sequence of 300 items should require seven-and-a-half hours. This information and other gleanings acquired from initial field tests of the first sequences equip the programmer with guideposts for more extensive field testing. Moreover, these data supply a rationale for separating the program into units more easily supervised in school situations.

ERROR ANALYSIS. From analysis of the responses comes the first information as to the possible effects of the program on the learner. If, for instance, there are one or more items to which everyone, nearly everyone, or a substantial majority of the learners responds erroneously, it is evident that the programmer has presented stimuli that do not evoke the responses he thought they should. For a teacher or industrial trainer this is a significant discovery. Why did it happen? There are several possible explanations.

Perhaps the programmer did not understand the subject matter as well as he should. Perhaps he did not make his assumptions about the learners as well as he might, or made some inaccurate assumptions based on insufficient evidence. Or he may have made an inexact translation from his objectives to the kinds of behavior needed to approximate his goals. Or he may have used a method of programming that does not afford him or the learners the opportunity to comprehend fully the stimulus-response relationships.

Before undertaking to rewrite the items, however, the programmer should inspect the nature of the responses. From them, he may discover how to improve the stimuli—and then test the items again with a larger number of learners. On the other hand, he may have to make a basic change in the program method or revise his estimates and assumptions about the learners' prior knowledge.

When the learners do not commit any errors on the program, the programmer might conclude that he had correctly developed the preliminary steps of the programming process. Yet the absence of error does not necessarily signify a good program. The important question is: Does the program enable learners to perform in accordance with the behavioral objectives stated by the programmer? If the majority of the learners can pursue the program with a minimum of error and the behaviors sought by the programmer can be easily discerned, the actual number of errors becomes a subsidiary matter. The essential value of noting the amounts and kinds of error really lies in the editing and refining of a program.

All this speculation and elucidation about error thus far applies only to linear types of programs. Certainly, if the erroneous response is corrected immediately and the learner continues to respond properly to subsequent items, the commission of the error per se is not of great importance to the building of a framework of learning. What may be useful to include in the description of a particular program is the average error-count for the learner group together with the range of error. A small distribution of error implies that no individual items account for all or most of the errors. It would seem, therefore, that a programmer would seek to produce sequences in which only a small distribution of errors occurs. Success in this respect indicates that editing has reached the point at which no groups of words or particular examples in their present form and order tend to cause a significant number of learners to respond incorrectly.

Awareness of the median in the distribution of errors among a group of learners also is valuable to the programmer. The median supplies another piece of information about the program's adequacy and provides a clearer clue as to how a typical student may be expected to perform on it. When the distribution of error is spread evenly over the range of errors, the median may be less important than when the distribution is *skewed*—that is, nonsymmetrical or uneven—but it nevertheless should be checked as part of the evaluation of the program.

In branching programs, error and numbers of errors assume a different meaning. Whereas in linear programs errors are attributed to the programmer and require a review of the items to eliminate them, errors are expected to occur in branching programs. The programmer recognizes that not all those exposed to the program necessarily have the identical background and ability. Consequently, he provides remedial items that branch out from the main stream of the program progression.[1] In such programs the data obtained from learners might suggest questions about the differences among them. Are those who make five or fewer errors more intelligent than the others who make more mistakes? Do learners who commit the most errors achieve poorly in other subjects and methods?

DIAGNOSTIC AND PRE-TEST DATA. Testing of learners for diagnostic purposes before building and using a program already has been explored in connection with instances in which the programmer wished to discover whether the learners had some specific knowledges and skills.[2] In a larger sense, the programmer might desire to construct an objective diagnostic test when there is no other way to be certain of the spread and extent of previous knowledge and skill for a program he might have in mind. For example, a programmer might want to devise a program in remedial arithmetic for seventh graders only to discover that nearly all the children had transferred into the present school system recently. It would seem, therefore, that he might begin

[1] For the details about branching, see Chapter 5, pp. 81–88.

[2] Chapter 3 describes the nature and function of the diagnostic test. See pp. 45–47.

by collecting data on them from some standardized test. He might, for instance, try the Iowa Tests of Basic Skills [3] which include four tests in Advanced Form for grades five through nine. One of these, Test D, deals with basic arithmetic skills. The other three cover matters of silent reading comprehension, and work-study and basic language skills. Not only would the test produce data capable of helping the programmer to establish where he should begin his program for this group, but it also could alert him to undertake a study of the range of performance to be included on the pre- and post-test inquiry.

He might ask himself these and other questions: Do those youngsters with a fairly homogeneous score—such as high on all four subjects—do the best on the program and the post-test? Do those who score high in basic arithmetic skills do well on the arithmetic remedial program regardless of their scores on the other tests?

The pre-testing of learners before they pursue a program and the post-testing after it produce data that can substantiate assertions about the value of the experience itself. Ideally, the objective pre- and post-tests should be equivalent, and they should be so constructed that the content and instructional aims of the program are best represented. One way to assure this is to design both tests from a two-way chart.[4] As shown in Figure 8-1, the subject content of the program is placed on the vertical axis and the instructional objectives on the horizontal axis. This example purposely is made abstract since almost any subject area could be organized this way. The important thing to realize is that the numbers in the cells represent numbers of items. This shows how much emphasis the programmer wishes to place on certain combinations of instructional objectives and content. The column at the right shows the relative emphasis in terms of content; the bottom row shows relative emphasis in terms of objectives. The total is 60 either way and serves as a computational check.

If two tests of 60 items each are constructed according to these

[3] *Iowa Every-Pupil Test of Basic Skills,* new edition, 1940–1950, Boston: Houghton Mifflin.

[4] Noll, Victor H., *Introduction to Educational Measurement,* Boston: Houghton Mifflin, 1957, p. 97f.

Program: (yours)

	Instructional Objectives				
	Knowledge & Understanding of		Ability to		
Content	Development & current status of	Relationships in field of	Apply correctly & interpret	Solve problems using	
Terminology	5	1	3	0	9
Specific facts	2	3	4	2	11
Rules and principles	3	3	4	1	11
Orders	1	2	3	1	7
Relationships	2	3	4	3	12
etc.	2	3	3	2	10
	15	15	21	9	60 total

Figure 8-1

specifications, there is a partial basis for saying that the tests are equivalent. They can be used before and after the program; and, if no other instruction has been provided, the net gain can be calculated. It is possible, moreover, especially when the program takes a month or more to pursue, to administer the same test before and after. **Then** the programmer can be certain as to equivalence of the two tests, but he might be wary lest the learners remember items from one administration of the test to the next.*

The net gain between tests may very well indicate that the program has helped the learners to learn—and in a successful program it will. Generally a statistical analysis of the test results will show that after exposure to the program the range of

* In some cases, such as mathematics, equivalence of the tests can be assured simply by changing numerical values in problems. This forestalls the possibility of remembering specific answers or solutions to items.

performance by the learners will be narrowed. That is to say, after programmed instruction, learners appear more alike.[5]

POST-TESTS AND OTHER CRITERIA. For the programmer, post-test results and other criteria of accomplishment, such as the ability to participate successfully in the next unit of study, aid in establishing whether the program actually accomplishes its mission. That is, the programmer can now appraise his unit selection criteria, his assumptions about his learners, his set of objectives, his choice of a program paradigm, and, perhaps, even the context in which all this activity has occurred. If he concludes that the program is very successful, he need not concern himself with further program improvement. For he might take on much more work than the gain is worth; the law of diminishing returns begins to operate. Perhaps he could turn more profitably to the programming of another unit while others try out his initial product.

If he finds, however, that the evaluation procedures do not show his program to be what he planned it to be, that it is still in need of editing and revision, he may re-examine each of the preparatory steps in relation to the results and possibly uncover some factor or factors that will enable him to make the required adjustments. He might wrestle with several pertinent questions.

With regard to the criteria for selection of a unit, did the criterion of *length* cause him to preclude the proper contextual materials from the program so that the facts, concepts, and skills sought were insufficiently supported? Did the criterion of *ease* cause him to overlook the necessity for sufficient repetition of significant concepts?

With regard to the assumptions about the learners, does he still find that his assumed characteristics of the learners are valid now that the program presumably has changed some of the motivational factors in learning with respect to the programmed material? In light of the lack of success of the program, do the learners need more maturity for real accomplishment in this subject? Does he now believe that he knows enough about the learners through the more traditional methods of gathering

[5] For two reasons why students might be expected to appear more alike, see Chapter 1, pp. 15–16.

data? Does he think that his lack of success has substantiated an already empirically demonstrated fact—that he has chosen a depressed area of learning because too much has always been expected of learners of this age range and experience?

With regard to the objectives of instruction, does the program build proper bases for those terminal behaviors previously selected? Did he include in his program all the behaviors selected as appropriate and provide practice in discrimination between the appropriate and inappropriate behaviors? Did he provide for practice in appropriate contexts so that the correct responses would follow the correct stimuli? Did he provide so complete an explanation of all the ideas and concepts that no challenge was felt by the learner?

With regard to the selection of a paradigm, does he now see that his choice fostered more recognition of information than recall? Does he now think that the selection of a linear paradigm penalized the creative thinkers? Would the inclusion of criterion frames in the program cause his evaluation to show more success? Does he now think, because his program deals with materials involving decision making and the development of judgment, that he should have selected a branching paradigm?

Hopefully, no new programmer will have to refer to the preceding material because of problems discovered in his unit. Nevertheless, even a weak start can be remedied and constitute a worthwhile learning experience for the beginner. In fact, a major contribution might be the willingness of individuals to share their failures as well as their successes so that all may increase their knowledge and, perhaps, forestall similar difficulties in the future.

The User's Problems

A *label* to accompany self-instructional programs has been proposed by Ernst Z. Rothkopf.[6] He believes the following items should be included with programs to assist others to assess their value:

[6] Rothkopf, Ernst Z., "A Suggested 'Label' for Self-Instructional Programs," from a paper read at the 26th Educational Conference, New York City, and included in *Aud.-Vis. Comm. Rev.*, Jan.–Feb., 1962, p. 63.

1. A complete copy of a performance test, including alternate forms, which represent the complete specification of the behavioral goals of the instructional program;

2. Specification of the student population used during evaluation: (a) number; (b) educational level and character (means and variability); (c) achievement levels (means and variability); (d) other predictor measures; e.g., reading proficiency;

3. Conditions of administration during evaluation: (a) group size and supervision; (b) incentive systems; (c) distribution of practice; (d) supplementary instruction; (e) other supplementary procedures such as laboratory exercises, demonstrations, films, etc.; (f) teaching machines which were used; (g) physical arrangements of room(s);

4. Results of evaluation: (a) performance test scores, means, variability, and relations to population characteristics such as I.Q.; (b) administration time as a function of population characteristics;

5. Recommendations for use;

6. Price;

7. Supplementary report describing the techniques used in the development of the program.

Most of these items constitute information about the relative success of the program under specified conditions. Presumably, the potential user can look at the title and this type of data and determine whether he wishes to try the program.

Because it is possible to develop a "strategy of programming" and because each of the preparatory steps contains several important details worthy of consideration in the programming process, it is desirable to include in the final report on the program the bases for all the decisions that have been made. The programmer, therefore, should provide information on all the following activities:

1. *Selection of unit.* What factor or factors caused him to select this particular unit? What data was analyzed in what manners to help in this selection? Were individuals with different competencies—subject-area specialists, educational psychologists, psychologists, teachers of the subject at the appropriate level, and trained programmers—consulted in the decision? Was this a committee decision?

2. *Assumptions about the learners.* Did the programmer try to make assumptions for the entire population of learners? Or did he just concern himself with the sample that was available? Was an attempt made to consider the combined data about the

learners? For instance, did certain background factors such as the educational level of the learners' parents cause the programmer to assume a certain vocabulary not consistent with reading test data?

3. *Selection of appropriate objectives.* What are the aims of the instructional program? Can an order indicating priority be established with these aims? Can those behaviors not desired be made less probable? Were others involved in the selection process? How? Was an attempt made to check the terminal behaviors against the response repertoires of the learners? How?

4. *Selection of a paradigm.* On what bases did he select his paradigm? Did he select it because of prior experience and, therefore, familiarity? Which factors in 1, 2, and 3 were considered in the paradigm selection? Was the mode of response in terminal behaviors a factor in his choice?

5. *Ordering and construction of items.* Was some method such as the RULEG or *mathetics* system used to order the items? What influenced the decision in this regard? Was it decided to use a combination of approaches? How was the decision made? What bases for a decision did he use to determine how much information to include in a given item, or the placement of the constructed response blank? If he chose a branching technique, did he use some rationale as an aid in constructing the multiple-choice questions? What was it?

6. *Editing and reviewing.* How were the learners selected for the initial field testing and editing? Was the subject-matter specialist called in at the beginning or during the process of editing and reviewing? As a result of this process how extensive were the changes and revisions?

7. *Evaluation.* What were the bases for the selection of the particular evaluation procedures? How were the pre- and post-tests developed? What information was compiled regarding the differing abilities and the different purposes of the learners? In what educational contexts were the programs field tested? In which of these were they most effective? How might the program best be used in a course?

These and many more questions are indicative of the substance that should be incorporated in the descriptions of a program. Indeed, *any additional information* which a user of a program can bring to bear towards the solution of some instructional problem will help, in the final analysis, to establish what has been accomplished and where the next step lies. The perplexing situation that most educators find themselves in regarding a decision to try auto-instructional materials will be lessened when more programs are accompanied by as complete information as possible.

In the meantime, until some measure of standardization can be established for the manual which should accompany each program, Rothkopf's label has merit if supplemented by three suggestions. First, in addition to his inclusion of a copy of a performance test, the programmer should list the desired *behavioral outcomes of instruction.* Second, the programmer should include the qualifications and experience of the reviewers and editors who aided the programmer in the process. These should be stipulated along with a complete specification of the student population. Third, he should attempt in each case to give the kinds of information indicated so that he can complete the description of the techniques used in the development of the program.

Although programming is still in the stage of comprehensive development as a technique and as a method of instruction to be used with the learners in our society, there may exist another area of programmer or publisher responsibility. Perhaps every program should be accompanied by a request—and facilities for answering [7]—for information gained from the program by a consumer. In this way, it would not be long before the author and the publisher of a program could accumulate data that might, when subjected to analysis, either reinforce the position already taken in the publication or cause some revision or rethinking of the particular instructional problem attacked by the program. Data regarding the effectiveness of a particular program might be shared by users and others so that soon a larger number of present and potential consumers would acquire the experiences on which to base a decision concerning its use.

If a consumer wished to carry on a simple experiment, he might offer the programmed unit to one class and administer his pre- and post-tests to that class and a second one. He would

[7] Robert N. Saveland of Ginn and Company has developed a program on *Earth-Sun Relations* and has printed an experimental edition. He has developed data-gathering instruments for an eleven-state trial.

choose as the second class one as similar as possible to the first. Diagrammatically, he would be doing what appears in Figure 8-2. Both groups would take the pre- and post-tests at the same time. After the results had been gathered and the descriptive data, such as the I.Q. or achievement scores, had been added to it, the user could begin to appraise the effectiveness of the programmed unit.

He could make a logical analysis of his data as already has been described.

He might compare the descriptive data for the two groups to test the assumption that they are very similar.

He might compare the post-test results to see if he can say, logically, that one group performed better than another.

He could compare the pre- and post-test results for each group to see if both of them improved during the course of instruction.

If the programmed unit is a standard unit of instruction and if there have been similar students studying it in the past the user may find that he already has data from some standard test, which is administered every year. In this case, he has for his convenience what some call an *historical control group* and he can compare that group's results with the group undergoing instruction via a program now.

The preceding suggestions are quite simple. Obviously they do not include the fine controls that professional researchers would desire. Because of this, the essential question for the instructor would be: Does the program cause the students to in-

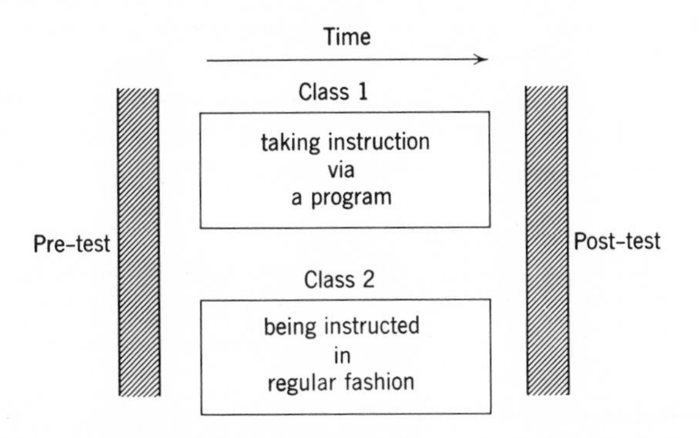

Figure 8-2

crease their knowledge and skills as specified by the objectives developed by the programmer? This question can be answered, of course, in some instances, even by as simple a means as teacher observations and student comments. In other cases, the teacher may wish to administer either his own test or those that accompany the program. If more sophisticated controls are desired, the instructor should solicit professional assistance.

In sum, evaluation is never an easy process to carry out. Approximations, however, offer different kinds of sets of data which can be used to help establish whether one type of instruction is more efficient than another. The important thing for most teachers, trainers, and professional programmers to remember is that evaluation should be a continuous process. When one concludes that there is nothing more to learn about certain processes in instruction and learning, one has ceased to advance.

SELECTED READINGS

1. Bloom, Benjamin S., et al., *Taxonomy of Educational Objectives—The Classification of Educational Goals Handbook I: The Cognitive Domain,* New York: Longmans, Green, 1956.

This book also contains sample test items along with the objectives.

2. Furst, Edward J., *Constructing Evaluation Instruments,* New York: Longmans, Green, 1958.

Chapter 8 contains a thorough treatment of problems in constructing various kinds of test items.

3. Ginther, John R., "A Model for Analyzing Programmed Materials," *Administrator's Notebook,* Vol. 10, No. 5, January, 1962, entire issue (4 pp.).

A description is presented of two dimensions of a three-dimensional model used for analyzing classroom instruction. The two dimensions, as applied to programmed learning, are a programming dimension with two poles (errorless to dialectical), and a mental process dimension (lower and higher).

4. Gotkin, Lassar, "Choosing a Program: How to Start," *Programed Instruction,* Vol. 1, No. 2, October, 1961, pp. 4 and 6.

Four questions considered: Is the content appropriate? Is the content well programmed? What have the students learned from the Program? What are the characteristics of the student population(s) involved in trial runs?

5. Holland, James G., "Evaluating Teaching Machines and Programs," *Teachers College Record,* Vol. 63, No. 1, October, 1961, pp. 56–65.

A number of helpful considerations with regard to programs, machines, and research are presented.

6. "A Joint Statement on Self-Instructional Materials and Devices," by Committees of the American Educational Research Association, the American Psychological Association, and the Department of Audio-Visual Instruction of the National Education Association, May, 1961. Distributed by the Department, NEA.

Eight guidelines to be used in evaluating programs.

7. Noll, Victor H., *Introduction to Educational Measurement,* Boston: Houghton Mifflin, 1957.

An excellent book on educational measurement for the beginner. Chapters 6 and 7 should prove helpful to the beginning programmer.

8. Thomas, R. Murray, *Judging Student Progress,* New York: Longmans, Green, 1960.

Should help teachers and others to organize an over-all evaluation system and develop appreciation for various kinds of achievement.

9. Wandt, Edwin, and Gerald W. Brown, *Essentials of Educational Evaluation,* New York: Henry Holt, 1957.

This inexpensive paperback book contains a concise treatment of the fundamentals of evaluation in the classroom.

Chapter

Nine

Applications and Implications

Throughout the course of these pages, the inclusion of many varied examples of programmed materials has shown that they can be introduced successfully at any level of instruction from the elementary grades through college and into the regions of adult and industrial education.* In the field of elementary education, programmed materials have enhanced the studies of the language arts, arithmetic, and life science, as well as the social studies and traffic safety. In high schools, they have been applied to English, foreign languages, science, social studies, health and physical education, business education, industrial arts, mathematics, driver education, and guidance. Colleges have employed them for work in nursing education, mathematics, the sciences, and business administration. Among adults and in industry, programs have been used for job training, office procedures, standard practices, mathematics, and supervisory training, to mention a handful of subjects.

Moreover, the commercial programs on the market illustrate beyond doubt that programmed instruction is useful at every

* If there is doubt about the motivational effects of the programmed method, they are quelled by the teacher who reported that a second grade pupil was so immersed in the program that after every correct response he leaped to his feet, clapped his hands, and shouted, "Hooray!" Happily, his classmates were so fully engrossed in their own programs that they paid little, if any, attention.

stage of the continuing educational process. Experimental work already has indicated its applicability at the pre-verbal level and in such areas as the instruction of retarded children. The function of this final chapter, therefore, is to assist the teacher or the training specialist to introduce programmed methods into instruction in order to improve the learning of his students and to utilize auto-instructional materials in the light of curriculum needs and special requirements, such as enrichment, remediation, and review.

Use of Programmed Materials

Although programs have proved their usefulness in every phase of education, over a period of time they very well might affect the internal arrangement of instructional procedure. Experiments already have raised significant questions about the conventional order and structure of the educational scheme.[1] Much of the literature to date, especially the statements of the purveyors of commercial programs, suggests that programs should be used basically as substitutes for the conventional method of teaching. In the Roanoke, Virginia, experiment on the application of programmed materials to the teaching of algebra, geometry, and trigonometry, the new method entirely replaced the conventional text, and the programs served largely as an alternative for the usual methods of instruction.[2]

Yet there are difficulties to be considered. Whereas pupils taught by programs generally evince a lower rate of failure than others taught by conventional means, in one case among a group of pupils studying algebra, one-fourth of the program users

[1] Rushton, E. W., "Programmed Learning in the Roanoke, Virginia, City School System," unpublished paper dated January 30, 1961. Eigen, L. D., and P. K. Komoski, "Automated Teaching Project Collegiate School," Research Summary No. 1, dated June, 1960, mimeo. McNamara, W. J., and J. L. Hughes, "IBM's Experience in Developing Programmed Instruction," Lysaught, J. P. (Ed.), *Programmed Learning: Evolving Principles and Industrial Applications,* Ann Arbor, Mich.: Foundation for Research on Human Behavior, 1961, pp. 53–57.

[2] "TEMAC Programmed Learning Materials, Report No. 2," Wilmette, Ill.: Encyclopaedia Britannica Films, April, 1961.

failed to pass a standardized algebra test in contrast to only 9 per cent of a conventional class. This glaring inconsistency urges caution in making claims for programmed matter. Rather than serving as a replacement for ordinary methods of instruction, programming might have more effectiveness when used in small units. It can be introduced gradually and used for specific purposes short of entirely superseding current instruction. A programmer may find it more prudent to begin in a modest way. By so doing, he will truly benefit from his work. He would do well to program short units to complement, enrich, remedy, and review other instruction.

COMPLEMENTATION. Both commercial programs and units developed by individual teachers can be used to complement instruction. That is to say, for a *given objective* a programmed bit can replace the customary form of instruction. The sequences may be employed for a few minutes a day for a brief period of time. In an elementary science course, for example, talks about cloud formations yield to a programmed sequence of 100 items. The unit may be used, evaluated, and revised all within two weeks.

Another means of complementing instruction is to introduce a brief sequence that exercises valuable skills not normally challenged by the curriculum. Multiplying by means of a slide rule, logic, and other tangential matters may be programmed to aid the students in their learning endeavors. The introduction of such programs does not interfere with the continuing instructional process while it contributes significant information and experience. Nor are mastery and retention of this knowledge likely to be affected by the other contents of the course.

ENRICHMENT. Enrichment units relate to the regular curriculum and provide enhanced understanding of it. They accord expanded learning opportunities for qualified students while allowing the teacher to give individual attention to all the students in his class. They do not pose any problems to the organization of the standard curriculum. Enrichment units might include both advanced subject matter and more problem-solving opportunities in the context of the regular curriculum.

REMEDIATION. Still another approach to introducing and utilizing programmed materials in the classroom is in the form of remedial exercises. An area of difficulty can be programmed to give learners encountering trouble with the conventional instructional procedure another opportunity to attack the subject matter. Short sequences suffice for these purposes and a number of them have been used to advantage in arithmetic and language skills. One possible benefit of such units is that over a period of time they might be revised and used for the initial instruction, and obviate the need for corrective measures.

REVIEW. One final way to add a programmed sequence is to apply it to the problem of review. Although review may be regarded as supplying assistance of a remedial type to students, there are times when a teacher does not know beforehand how much repetitive material to include in his instructional plans. In such cases, a review of portions of previous instruction illuminates the situation. Programmed sequences work well at these moments. Pressey has urged the consistent, coordinated use of programs as an adjunct to regular instruction; that is, all students would use auto-instructional materials as a review in the normal operation of the curriculum.[3]

Administration of Programs

Most experimental use in auto-instructional learning has occurred in the classroom during the regular period of instruction for the particular subject matter. This has the advantage of making the teacher available for individual assistance should the learner run into difficulty or have a question about an extension of the programmed material. In other words, the teacher can supplement the programmed exercise.

Nevertheless, there are other fruitful ways to employ a program. It may be used as part of the learner's homework, both to review the work previously covered by traditional instruction

[3] Pressey, S. L., "Basic Unresolved Teaching-Machine Problems," *Theory Into Practice,* Vol. I, No. 1, Columbus, O.: Bureau of Educational Research and Service, Ohio State University, February, 1962.

and to prepare for the next lessons. Such usage has been beneficial at every educational level.[4] Another approach to the administration of programmed learning is to make it available on the school or industrial plant premises, but to locate it apart from the scene of the regular occupations. Such self-instruction laboratories centralize the use of programmed materials which learners may pursue whenever they have the time, but a teacher is not likely to be on tap to help them, if assistance is needed. However, there is as yet no concrete evidence that a teacher has to be present while a student uses a program, even though most teachers, during this exploratory stage in the employment of programmed materials, probably would prefer maximum involvement for their own information and evaluation.[5]

Programs also have been administered to single learners with the students conferring face to face with a teacher only as questions or problems arise. A rural school in upstate New York, for instance, does not regularly offer a course in trigonometry because fewer than five students would want it. Aided by programmed materials, the algebra teacher has three students working on trigonometry. They pursue units both at school and at home, and drop into the teacher's office individually as they need assistance or as they complete sections and are ready to take achievement tests which the teacher prepares.

Irrespective of how the teacher chooses to administer a program, he must provide adequate instructions on the use of the materials to his pupils. He may do so orally, explaining the procedures to be followed in constructing or selecting a response, in moving to the next appropriate item, or in handling of errors; but it is preferable to commit these instructions to writing so that other teachers in using the program may be able to pass all the necessary information to their learners. For research purposes, of course, the record of directions given to learners is most important.

[4] "Implementation Studies," *Programed Instruction,* Center for Programed Instruction, Vol. I, No. 4, February, 1962, p. 3. Blyth, J. W., "Teaching Machines and Human Beings" (Lumsdaine and Glaser, pp. 404–406). Lysaught, J. P., "Industrial Training Through Programmed Learning," *Personnel Journ.,* Vol. 40, No. 4, September, 1961, pp. 165–169.

[5] TEMAC, *op. cit.* It was indicated that there was no advantage detected between groups which receive "help" and "no-help" from the teacher.

Some programmers have gone further and built these directions for using a program into their initial units. This not only provides guidance, but also prepares learners for proper handling of the unit by assuring the actual manipulation of the programmed process. There is one other merit in programming the directions. Students often require a certain amount of adjustment to become acquainted with the programming technique. An introductory section that explains the program facilitates the adjustment before the subject matter is reached. For this reason, there are those programmers who have devised short units to "break the ice" before the administration of a program designed to complement or enrich a course of instruction.

Role of the Teacher

The entire focus of this book has stressed the involvement of the classroom teacher or the training specialist in every phase of the programming process. As John Barlow has said: "I have some real reservations as to the overall profit to the student and to education in instances in which a teacher who has never constructed a program and who does not understand the process involved in them, uses programs for his students that someone else has prepared for him."[6] And as Alice Foley of the New York State Teachers Association has written: "I am certain that any teacher who does some programming will be a better teacher when he has finished his work."[7] The teacher's role is one of dynamic participation, of constructing units, trying them out, and being part of the developing experience.

What of the teacher's role, then, with respect to commercial programs, or even in relations to units programmed by other teachers? It is just as important in these situations that the teacher play an active part. In weighing someone else's programmed materials for his own use, the teacher should be guided by the factors outlined in the programming process. To the ex-

[6] *Programed Instruction,* Center for Programed Instruction, Vol. 1, No. 1, May, 1961, p. 3.

[7] Lysaught, J. P., "Programmed Learning and the Classroom Teacher," *New York State Education,* February, 1961, p. 11.

tent that he has had programming experience, he will find it easier to assess a program's value. In many commercial programs he will discover a lack of information on how the unit has been tested and what results have been obtained. He can compensate this deficiency by setting up a limited field trial in order to evaluate the program and its effectiveness.

In the use of programs, there seems to be considerable confusion over the function of the teacher. Many critics of programming have suggested that the teacher will be supplanted by the program or the machine. The proponents of programmed learning have countered with assurances that the teacher will not be eliminated. Most likely, the truth of the matter falls somewhere between. The program and the machine will not replace the teacher, but any responsible appraisal of their effect indicates that the role of the teacher may very well change.

A teacher faced with the needs of a number of pupils, each of them working at his optimum rate, is challenged to apply effective, personalized tutorial assistance to each pupil at the point where the learner actually is—not at the point where he might or should be. With the aid of the learning program, the teacher can devote a much larger part of his time to counseling, guiding, assisting, and stimulating the individual learners. In reflecting on these possibilities, Harry Broudy has commented: "If the teacher is a source of non-standardized insights; if the teacher is creative enough to produce a highly personal reaction to the world and to the subjects he teaches, then he is a valuable asset and not a machine at all."[8] The implication is clear. If certain classroom tasks can be accomplished by a machine, then they should be done by the machine, and not by the human being. The human being, the classroom teacher, should do those things the machine cannot do. In the process, teacher, learner, and learning all will benefit.

Then there is this final aspect of the altered role of the classroom teacher who uses learning programs. Necessarily, the teacher must take an experimental, pragmatic approach to the learning process. He must test out programs, and hopefully construct and try sequences of his own. In so doing, he will find

[8] Broudy, Harry S., *Paradox and Promise,* Englewood Cliffs, N.J.: Prentice-Hall, 1961, pp. 153–154.

himself drawn closer to the realities of learning, and to the behavior of the learner caught up in the process. He will observe that he is constantly testing his assumptions about learners against the facts of their actual learning patterns. He will discover himself recognizing and squaring up to the truth that some sequences will succeed while some will fail; but the analysis of success or failure will produce still greater insight into his own role and the role of the learner. If programmed learning accomplished nothing more than putting the spotlight on the behaviors of teaching and learning, the efforts of the individual teacher or training specialist in developing programmed materials would be amply repaid.

The Learning Program and the Learner

In a recent survey of more than 30 research studies on programmed learning, Jack Quackenbush found evidence that the generalizations about the effectiveness of the method have been proven in classroom applications.[9] Students pursuing programs, for instance, scored higher on standardized achievement tests than did fellow students taught by conventional classroom methods. Variations in the individual rates of learning through programmed units were confirmed. Similarly, decreases in the predictability of student performance were demonstrated—that is, students were making more progress than might have been expected, or they were mastering material that ordinarily might have been considered beyond their level of comprehension.

Although such studies are encouraging, it should be noted in the interest of objectivity that most of the reported experiences concerned a limited number of students, often from a relatively select category, using a single program, in one subject matter, and usually for a limited period of time. It might be unwise to generalize too much from the findings, but their value certainly cannot be ignored. Significantly, the students evinced only a minimum of unfavorable reaction to programmed learning in

[9] Quackenbush, Jack, "How Effective Are the New Auto-Instructional Materials and Devices?" *IRE Tran. on Educ.*, No. 4, December, 1961, pp. 144–151.

all the studies Quackenbush surveyed. Perhaps even more revealing is the character of the discontent expressed. Some students were bored; others thought that the program so simplified the understanding of the material that they were disappointed at not encountering greater difficulty. The first problem obviously calls for better programming. The second points to the need for a more imaginative development of the program sequences so that they will challenge the student's learning ability.*

One further consideration with respect to the learner and the learning program is that there is a substantial redefinition of the student's role in the learning process. Not only is there active interaction between the student and the sequence, but there is also the fact that student achievement is essentially the measure of the program's utility. This is a decided contrast to the notion that scholastic achievement is the measure of the student. The significance is clear. The learner is now central to the educational process; if he errs, the programmer must accommodate his own behavior to the facts of the student's response and endeavor to improve the program's learning pattern. Thus, the burden is at least equally shared by the teacher and the learner—and that is how most excellent teachers always have viewed it. In many classrooms, however, the facts of life are that students simply pass or fail. Programmed learning constitutes a powerful new instrument to discern how successful and unsuccessful students behave, and to recommend how to make students more successful by providing better guides to the objective.

In addition to redefining the student's role in the learning process, programming will open new opportunities for exploration to him. As programs live up to their promise, students no longer are limited by the standard perimeter of the learning environment. The student who attends a high school where statistics are not taught can now obtain an insight and skill of a higher order than might be realistically acquired from reading

* Another possible explanation for student disinterest may be that some programs were intended for experimentation rather than instruction. Generally students are quick to recognize the difference, and to react if the material does not meet their own goals.

a textbook on his own initiative. Programmed learning through careful sequencing, active involvement, and reinforcement makes the learner a partner to the development of his own future, thereby ending his existence as a passive subject to be acted upon.

The Curriculum and the Learning Process

It should not be surprising that programmed learning has discernible impacts on the standard curriculum. Two of these are to be seen in existing research, as fragmentary as it may be. The Quackenbush survey, for instance, noted that subjects taught traditionally at certain age and grade levels could be learned effectively by younger children in lower grades if presented through programmed materials, and that variability in the student learning rate increased so much as a result of programmed instruction that traditional time periods for the mastery of material were rendered meaningless.[10]

The first of these impacts raises questions about the customary progression of subject matter and the beliefs regarding the readiness of students to learn in the conventional curriculum. If it can be shown by programmed instruction that elementary pupils can master course matter in statistics normally taught in college, both teacher and administrator at several levels in the educational system must face some harsh realities and meet them with relevant answers. Is there any value to be gained by an elementary pupil from learning something about statistics? If there is, and if the pupil can master at least important parts of the subject matter, what happens to the traditional arrangement of subjects in the field of mathematics in grade school, high school, and college? Is there a logical defense for the present structure of exposures to learning, or is it simply a matter of "that is the way it has always been done"? On the other hand, is it possible that there is really no value for the pupil to learn statistics in the elementary grades? There certainly would be little value in terms of the laws of use and disuse if the student

[10] Quackenbush, *op. cit.*

were to learn something about statistics and never use the knowledge until he reached college. This would not make much sense in logic or practicality.

Many questions are being asked these days with regard to the structure of educational experiences in our school systems. Some of them stem from the reappraisals undertaken by educators and others since the Soviets put their Sputnik satellite into orbit. Other questions have been churning among the members of various disciplines—physics is one example—as they have tried to rearrange the sequence and content of courses to improve the learning process. Programmed learning does not impose new problems on the educational scene, but it may provide a means for sharpening the answers to those problems that already exist.

Similarly, the highlighting of the individual variation in learning, which programmed learning emphasizes, is not a unique result of this new methodology. Educators have been at work on the problem for some time. Proposals have been made, for instance, that large groups, small groups, and individual study be used more extensively, and that the general adherence to normal-sized classes be reduced. Programmed learning, in this sense, could become a vital device in the exercise of individual study, which most educators recognize as being at the heart of any basic changes in the system.

Perhaps the day will come when the ungraded classroom and the individual progress of the student through a series of educational experiences adjusted to his capabilities and capacities will be the distinctive mark of American education. If this comes about, it will be in large part because programmed instruction is practiced effectively. For the long run, then, programmed instruction is a vehicle for effectuating changes that might be desired in the organization of the curriculum, and for the progress of the individual student through that structure. Students can learn traditional arithmetic from a program; they also can learn the sets, relations, and functions of modern mathematics. It is the responsibility of the school and the teacher to determine which a student will learn—and when. Possibly through the use of self-instructional materials, the student can gain the time and capacity to participate more vigorously in the decision-making process within the educational system.

State of the Programming Art

Programming and teaching by means of programs are still in the early, exhilarating stage of exploration.[11] Much has been done, but much more remains. Although the future is filled with promise, some nagging problems already have manifested themselves. Among them are the following: First, inflexible thinking with respect to programming paradigms; some feel that only the Skinner or only the Crowder model is acceptable for teaching purposes. The authors have attempted to suggest a pragmatic approach utilizing many kinds of models suited to the various learning situations a programmer experiences. Second, a growing controversy over teaching machines versus programmed textbooks, without proper study and evaluation of the applications of each to the total sequence of learning experiences. Third, the increased use of jargon in connection with programmed learning—and the consequent distress of teachers and others who believe that this adds unnecessary complications to the gaining of understanding. Fourth, an undue emphasis on the role of the behavioral psychologist in the development of a learning program; occasionally it is implied that only the psychologist can program learning material. Fifth, a corollary to the previous problem: teachers cannot or should not write programs.

All these problems emerge from broad and careless generalizations made on the basis of insufficient research evidence. In many cases, they represent the vested interests of individuals and groups. In the experience of the authors, at least, it seems obvious that a large number of programming paradigms are acceptable. Likewise, there are reasons for using teaching machines in one application and preferring programmed textbooks in another, as will be explained presently. Certain terms are important in programmed learning for precision in expression, but words, after all, are meant to communicate; if jargon interferes with understanding, it is the jargon that must be changed, not the learner. And, finally, although the psychologist can

[11] Lysaught, J. P., "A Commentary on the State of the Art," *AID,* November, 1961, pp. 66–7.

contribute heavily to the development of good programs, he does not have an exclusive franchise in the field; the teacher, academic, industrial, or military, can and must, in the opinion of the authors, be involved in program construction.

Teaching Machines

Because it was the teaching machine that early caught the fancy of many general readers, it is not surprising that a large part of the first literature in the field of programmed learning tends to stress the mechanical developments at the expense of the learning content to be presented to the student. Undoubtedly this misplaced emphasis awakened much of the public interest in programmed learning, and just as certainly placed many educators on the defensive. Time has swung the balance. If the public has become disenchanted because teaching machines are not to be found in every classroom, many educators have begun to discover that behind the machine stands a significant body of learning theory and research.*

Since the 1920's applications of technology have been explored on a broad front. In 1960, for example, it was estimated that educational institutions of all kinds spent $103,000,000 for audio-visual equipment and materials.[12] Included in these purchases were such articles as slide projectors, motion-picture projectors, opaque and overhead projectors, language laboratories, and tape- and record-playing equipment. In a broad sense, each of these devices is a machine designed to teach although it may not be readily apparent how they differ from the machines developed from programmed learning. Some of them, in fact,

* The nadir of the public understanding of teaching machines, no doubt, is the school administrator who asked for a recommendation from a group of experienced programmers on which machines to buy. Told that this would depend on how he planned to use the machines, he confessed that he did not want to do anything with them, but that he and his school board intended to keep up the school's reputation for experimenting in "new methods" and twenty machines in a room would assure the PTA that the school was up-to-date.

[12] Flory, J., and T. W. Hope, "Non-Theatrical Films—Interim Report No. 2," *Journ. of the SMPTE,* Vol. 70, January, 1961.

can be used as components of a teaching machine for auto-instruction—as, for example, a tape player—or may be modified to perform the functions of a programmed teaching machine, as in the case of the slide projector.

The most important difference between bonafide teaching machines and the plethora of audio-visual devices lies in their relation to the stimulus-response cycle. The true teaching machine covers the whole stimulus-response mechanism, including *feedback,* reinforcement, and extinction,[13] whereas the other devices when modified or adapted affect only a portion of the complete learning process. The teaching machine lays a learning program before a student. As such, it should provide several services. First, it must present *programmed input:* that is, material arranged in a series of small, gradual steps designed to move the student from a familiar background into a complex of new principles, concepts, and understandings. Second, it must engage in *stimulus presentation* of the items in the program in accordance with the programmer's paradigm. Third, it must elicit the *required response* on the part of the student, although this may vary as to form and manner. Fourth, it must supply *immediate feedback* to the student as to the adequacy and correctness of a response. Fifth, it must offer *reinforcement or extinction* on the basis of the feedback.

Most authorities would agree on these requirements for a teaching machine.[14] Others, however, prefer further refinements in these characteristics. Among them, Lawrence Stolurow distinguishes between *non-adaptive* machines, which would meet the foregoing minimum requirements, and *adaptive* machines, which also would include the five following features: *pacing*—that is, the control of important time variables, such as the time between presentation of the stimulus and presentation of the program response; *collator-recorder*—that is, the assemblage

[13] Porter, Douglas, "A Critical Review of a Portion of the Literature on Teaching Devices," *Harvard Educ. Rev.,* Vol. XXVII, No. 2, Spring, 1957, pp. 126–147 (Lumsdaine and Glaser, pp. 114–132).

[14] Finn, J. D., "Technology and the Instructional Process," *Phi Delta Kappan,* XLI, No. 9, June, 1960. Porter, Douglas, "Teaching Machines," *Harv. Grad. School of Education Assn. Bull.,* Vol. 3, March, 1958 (Lumsdaine and Glaser, p. 206). Lumsdaine, A. A., "Some Issues Concerning Devices and Programs for Automated Learning" (Lumsdaine and Glaser, p. 517).

of such data as numbers and types of error, or time intervals; *selector*—that is, the ability to select succeeding items of the program based on student performance, proficiency, and the like; *library*—that is, the storage of information to be used as needed by the learner, and *computer*—that is, utilization of electronic means to carry out the storage, selection, collation, and other provisions within the system.[15]

Clearly, a spectrum of teaching machine complexity could be constructed with the programmed textbook at one end and a computer-based electronic system at the other. Between them would lie a number of distinguishable approaches—the sliding mask, the sheet-paper device, the roll-paper mechanism, the film or microfilm machine, and the electric or electronic unit which can accommodate several of the additional characteristics proposed for adaptive machines. The questions are: Are these machines really necessary for the utilization of learning programs? Are they desirable for classrooms? And what are the essential considerations in deciding how to use them?

NECESSARY? At one end of the spectrum of acceptable teaching machines, as was noted, stands the programmed textbook. Strictly speaking, it may not qualify literally as a teaching machine, but it possesses the capacity to present programmed stimuli to a student and follow through the remaining steps in the learning cycle. As might be anticipated, and has been observed in passing earlier in the chapter, a controversy has developed over the need for a machine when a book can accomplish the task.

There is little doubt that much programmed material can be transmitted through the agency of the programmed textbook, or the scrambled textbook that is used to present intrinsically programmed lessons. Two studies have reported that "the teaching machine simulator (the programmed textbook) is just as adequate a teaching device as a teaching machine itself."[16] A number of other studies which used only the programmed text-

[15] Stolurow, L. M., *Teaching by Machine,* Co-operative Research Monograph No. 6, U.S. Department of Health, Education, and Welfare, 1961, pp. 6–16.
[16] Eigen, L. D., and P. K. Komoski, "Research Summary No. 1, Collegiate School Automated Teaching Project," New York: Center for Programed Instruction, 1960, mimeo.

book have indicated that students learn well by following a program without the benefit of a mechanical teaching device.[17] From these and other researches[18] the evidence seems to suggest that the teaching machine per se is not an absolute necessity for learning programs in the classroom—possibly because neither program development nor research is far enough advanced to identify the pertinent factors in machine utilization.

Nevertheless, some indications certainly exist that a form of teaching machine may be required for some applications of programmed learning. In his study of the "temporal patterning of behavior called 'rhythm,'" Skinner employs an audio-stimulus teaching machine which would be impossible to duplicate on the printed page.[19] And there are likely to be programs at the nonverbal or exceptional child levels that would be hard to handle by means of a programmed text.

From the standpoint of the programmer or the teacher confronted by normal classroom demands, however, the programmed textbook is indeed sufficient. For the majority of purposes neither the programmer nor the teacher is likely to find the teaching machine necessary for classroom use.

DESIRABLE? In shifting from necessity to desirability the answers to the question become less positive. Essentially, the issue of desirability comes down to the individual learning situation and the preferences of the programmer or teacher. In general, for the short run, the weight of evidence to date seems to favor initial use of the programmed textbook, or the scrambled textbook. Over a longer haul, however, as more materials become available for use, and as their composition acquires more complexity, the point may be reached at which mechanical devices

17 Smith, W., and J. W. Moore, "Size-of-Step and Achievement in Programmed Spelling," Bucknell University, September, 1961. Reproduced in Smith and Moore, *Programmed Learning,* New York: Van Nostrand, 1962. Allen, L. E., "Progress Report of the ALL Project," Yale, Oct. 15, 1961. Alexander, H. W., and R. F. Smith, "A Self-Instruction Program in Elementary Statistics," Earlham College, 1961, mimeo.

18 Lysaught, J. P., and C. M. Williams, "A Community Explores Programmed Learning, Parts I & II," NYS *Education,* February and March, 1962.

19 Skinner, B. F., "Why We Need Teaching Machines," *Cumulative Record,* enlarged edition, New York: Appleton-Century-Crofts, 1961, pp. 182.04–5.

become quite desirable, if not absolutely necessary. Even now, there are certain applications that dictate the desirability of machines to follow the programming model.

There is another factor to be considered although the evidence is so inconclusive as to make generalizations futile. This is the matter of attitude toward the use of a teaching machine on the part of both the instructor and the learner. Some reactions are positive; reports favor programmed materials presented by machine as "more absorbing" and "more demanding." Other reactions are negative to the machine while favorable to the program content. To some extent, the latter attitude may be attributed to mechanical and design deficiencies in early machine models.[20] Until more evidence becomes available, the proper approach might be one of sympathetic caution, of using known techniques pending exposure of their limitations or signs of established improvements.

RESEARCH. As a research tool, the teaching machine comes into its own, particularly in fundamental research on the nature of reinforcement theory and program models. Among the factors to be assayed in determining whether it should be used in research work are its ability to control, its facility to record, its flexibility, and its cost.

Better understanding of the reinforcement cycle requires precise control over the presentation of the stimuli and the resulting responses. Part of this control easily could be the capacity to vary the duration, magnitude, and object-field relationship of the stimulus. Better control over the response behavior of the learner likewise is vital. The machine can cope with all this and it also has the ability to vary the nature and frequency of reinforcement.

For research purposes, more data needs to be recorded and analyzed than generally is gathered for field testing. Accurate records of responses are needed to distinguish substantive from procedural mistakes. In some instances, elapsed time in responding should be recorded to be compared with errors and the content of the items. Responses to intrinsic programs must be

[20] Lysaught, J. P., "Industrial Training Through Programmed Learning," *Personnel Journ.*, September, 1961.

recorded to reconstruct the learning process followed by the student. All these things the machine can do.

Research equipment has to have the flexibility to vary the programming paradigm or model. It must, moreover, have sufficient facilities for stimulus and response modes, including audio, visual, and tactual capacities. All of which a teaching machine has in addition to possessing the internal library storage and memory systems required for investigations involving complex programming and adaptive branches.

Because a research device requires many features which never may be needed in a classroom device, the cost consideration is much different. The teaching machine for the student, in all likelihood, always will remain a compromise between efficiency and economy. On the other hand, to learn how to increase the effectiveness of programmed learning, research equipment must be chosen primarily from the standpoint of the work to be done and the tools needed to do it.

Basic research on programmed learning, it would seem apparent from these considerations, requires the use of complicated devices and equipment just as Skinner's research on reinforcement theory necessitated complex apparatus and associated recording devices.[21] Nor is it unreasonable to expect that further investigation into human learning will require more sophisticated manipulative and measuring tools than similar research on lower organisms. Quite possibly the widespread introduction of teaching machines into the classroom may be a direct function of the development of adequate, research devices.

Of some things, we may be sure. Many prolonged studies are going to be necessary to produce balanced conclusions about the final value of programmed instruction, as promising as the evidence has been thus far. Similarly, the jury will be out for some time on the fate of the teaching machine in its suit to be an adjunct of the programming process. In the meantime, improved programming techniques are certain to appear, new uses for programming are bound to develop, and the programs of today are likely to be fossilized by the programs of tomorrow.

[21] An interesting film of Skinner's laboratory work is "Learning and Behavior," 30 min., 16mm sound, b&w, available from Carousel Films, New York City. (See also Bibliography, Section F.)

What is most needed now is for more teachers, more schools, and more learners to gain experience in the use of programmed materials, and to share their findings with others. Voluntary cooperation, extended field study, resistance to overgeneralization, and the yearning to experiment—these are the avenues to progress. The future contains unanswered questions, but the performance to the present time shows that the capability for discovering the solutions is indeed at hand.

SELECTED READINGS

1. Coulson, John E. (Ed.), *Programmed Learning and Computer-Based Instruction,* New York: John Wiley and Sons, 1962.

A collection of papers on the application of digital computers to automated instruction.

2. Finn, James D., and Donald G. Perrin, *Teaching Machines and Programmed Learning, 1962: A Survey of the Industry,* Occasional Paper No. 3, Washington, D.C.: NEA, 1962.

An illustrated listing of teaching machines including both those commercially available at present and those under research and field testing.

3. Galanter, Eugene (Ed.), *Automatic Teaching: The State of the Art,* New York: John Wiley and Sons, 1959.

Briggs, Leslie J., "Teaching Machines for Training of Military Personnel in Maintenance of Electronic Equipment," pp. 131–145.

Porter, Douglas, "Some Effects of Year Long Teaching Machine Instruction," pp. 85–90.

4. Lumsdaine, Arthur A., and Robert Glaser (Eds.), *Teaching Machines and Programmed Learning: A Source Book,* Washington, D.C.: NEA, 1960.

Blyth, John W., "Teaching Machines and Human Beings," pp. 401–415.

Ferster, Charles B., and Stanley M. Sapon, "An Application of Recent Developments in Psychology to the Teaching of German," pp. 173–185.

Keislar, Evan R., "The Development of Understanding in Arthmetic by a Teaching Machine," pp. 425–436.

All the papers listed from Galanter and from Lumsdaine and Glaser are short reports of programmed learning applications.

5. Lumsdaine, Arthur A., and Robert Glaser (Eds.), *Teaching Machines and Programmed Learning: A Source Book,* Washington, D.C.: NEA, 1960.

Mellan, Ibert, "Teaching and Educational Inventions," pp. 265–274.

Porter, Douglas, "A Critical Review of a Portion of the Literature on Teaching Devices," pp. 114–132.

Ramo, Simon, "A New Technique of Education," pp. 367–381.

The articles by Mellan and Porter are often quoted as early compilations and analyses of automated teaching devices. The paper by Ramo is a classic prediction of the school for the future.

6. Margulies, Stuart, and Lewis D. Eigen (Eds.), *Applied Programed Instruction,* New York: John Wiley and Sons, 1962.

Hughes, J. L., "The Effectiveness of Programed Instruction: Experimental Findings," pp. 44–49.

Lysaught, Jerome P., "Programed Learning and Teaching Machines in Industrial Training," pp. 23–43.

These and other papers contained in the source describe adult and industrial applications of programmed learning.

7. Margulies, Stuart, and Lewis D. Eigen (Eds.), *Applied Programed Instruction,* New York: John Wiley and Sons, 1962.

Eigen, Lewis D., "Pseudo-Programed-Instruction Systems," pp. 241–252.

Foltz, Charles I., "Aids to Teaching: A Survey of the Current Status of Teaching Machines," pp. 219–240.

Klaus, David J., and Arthur A. Lumsdaine, "Some Economic Realities of Teaching-Machine Instruction," pp. 198–207.

Levine, Stanley L., and William J. Knight, "Teaching Machines for General and Special Purposes," pp. 277–280.

Silvern, Leonard C., "The Influence of Teaching-Machine Technology on Electronic-System Maintenance Training," pp. 253–276.

The papers discuss many considerations in the design and use of teaching machines,and the article by Klaus and Lumsdaine cuts to the heart of the economic question of machine utilization.

8. *Programs, '62—A Guide to Programed Instructional Materials Available to Educators by September 1962,* The Center for Programed Instruction, New York, in cooperation with the U.S. Department of Health, Education, and Welfare, Washington, D.C., 1962.

An informative reference to the kinds and varieties of programmed material.

9. Quackenbush, Jack, "How Effective Are the New Auto-Instructional Materials and Devices?" *IRE Trans. on Educ.,* No. 4, December, 1961, pp. 144–151.

A concise summary of reported research on applications of programmed learning in a variety of educational situations.

Selected Bibliography

A. BOOKS

Austwick, Kenneth (Ed.), *Teaching Machines and Programming,* New York: Macmillan Co., 1964.

Bartz, Albert E., *Elementary Statistical Methods for Educational Measurement,* Minneapolis: Burgess, 1958.

Becker, James L., *A Programed Guide to Writing Auto-Instructional Programs,* Camden, N. J.: RCA Service Company, 1963.

Bloom, Benjamin S., et al., *Taxonomy of Educational Objectives—The Classification of Educational Goals Handbook I: The Cognitive Domain,* New York: Longmans, Green, 1956.

Brethower, Dale M., *Programed Instruction: A Manual of Programing Techniques,* Chicago: Educational Methods, 1963.

———, D. G. Markle, G. A. Rummler, A. W. Schrader, and D. E. P. Smith, *Programmed Learning: A Practicum,* Ann Arbor, Michigan: Ann Arbor Publishers, 1965.

Broudy, Harry S., *Paradox and Promise,* Englewood Cliffs, N. J.: Prentice-Hall, 1961.

Coulson, John E. (Ed.), *Programmed Learning and Computer-Based Instruction,* New York: John Wiley and Sons, 1962.

Cram, David, *Explaining "Teaching Machines" and Programming,* San Francisco: Fearon, 1961.

Dale, Edgar, *Audio-Visual Methods in Teaching,* revised edition, New York: Henry Holt, 1959.

DeCecco, John P. (Ed.), *Educational Technology,* New York: Holt, Rinehart and Winston, 1964.

Deterline, William A., *An Introduction to Programed Instruction,* New York: Prentice-Hall, 1962.

Dolmatch, Theodore B., Elizabeth Marting, and Robert E. Finley

(Eds.), *Revolution in Training: Programed Instruction in Industry,* New York: American Management Association, 1962.

Epstein, Sam and Beryl, *The First Book of Teaching Machines,* New York: Franklin Watts, 1961.

Filep, Robert T. (Ed.), *Prospectives in Programming,* New York: Macmillan Co., 1963.

Fine, Benjamin, *Teaching Machines,* New York: Sterling, 1962.

Foltz, Charles I., *The World of Teaching Machines,* Washington, D.C.: Electronic Teaching Laboratories, 1961.

French, Will, et al., *Behavioral Goals of General Education in High School,* New York: Russell Sage Foundation, 1957.

Fry, Edward B., *Teaching Machines and Programmed Learning,* New York: McGraw-Hill, in press.

Furst, Edward J., *Constructing Evaluation Instruments,* New York: Longmans, Green, 1958.

Galanter, Eugene (Ed.), *Automatic Teaching: The State of the Art,* New York: John Wiley and Sons, 1959.

Glaser, Robert (Ed.), *Teaching Machines and Programmed Learning, II: Data and Directions,* Washington, D.C.: National Education Association, 1965.

Green, Edward J., *The Learning Process and Programmed Instruction,* New York: Holt, Rinehart & Winston, 1962.

Guest, Lester, *Beginning Statistics,* New York: Crowell, 1958.

Guthrie, W. K. C., *Plato, Protagoras and Meno,* Baltimore: Penguin Books, 1956.

Hayakawa, S. I., *Language in Thought and Action,* New York: Harcourt, Brace, 1949.

Hendershot, C. H. (Ed.), *Programmed Learning: A Bibliography of Programs and Presentation Devices* (Offset), University Center, Michigan: Delta College (Quarterly).

Hilgard, Ernest R., *Theories of Learning,* second edition, New York: Appleton-Century-Crofts, 1956.

Holland, James G., and B. F. Skinner, *The Analysis of Behavior,* New York: McGraw-Hill, 1961.

Holtz, Herman R., and Paul A. Alter, *A Short Course in Intrinsic Programming,* Silver Spring, Md.: U.S. Industries, 1965.

Hughes, John L., *Programed Instruction for Schools and Industry,* Chicago: Science Research Associates, 1962.

———, *Programmed Learning: A Critical Evaluation,* Chicago: Educational Methods, 1963.

Jacobs, Paul I., Milton H. Maier, and Laurence M. Stolurow, *A Guide to Evaluating Self-Instructional Programs,* New York: Holt, Rinehart and Winston, 1966.

Kearney, Nolan C., *Elementary School Objectives,* New York: Russell Sage Foundation, 1953.

Keller, Fred S., *Learning: Reinforcement Theory,* New York: Random House, 1954.

Korzybski, Alfred H., *Science and Sanity: An Introduction to Non-*

Aristotelian Systems and General Semantics, Lancaster, Pa.: Science Press, 1933.

Krathwohl, David A., et al., *Taxonomy of Educational Objectives—The Classification of Educational Goals: Handbook II: Affective Domain,* New York: David McKay, 1964.

Krauss, Ruth, *A Hole Is to Dig,* New York: Harper, 1952.

Lindgren, Henry C., *Educational Psychology in the Classroom,* New York: John Wiley and Sons, 1962.

Lindquist, E. F. (Ed.), *Educational Measurement,* Washington, D.C.: American Council on Education, 1951.

Lindvall, C. M. (Ed.), *Defining Educational Objectives.* A report of the Regional Commission on Educational Coordination and the Learning Research and Development Center, Pittsburgh: University of Pittsburgh Press (Paperback), 1964.

Lumsdaine, Arthur A., and Robert Glaser (Eds.), *Teaching Machines and Programmed Learning: A Source Book,* Washington, D.C.: National Education Association Department of Audio-Visual Instruction, 1960.

Lysaught, Jerome P. (Ed.), *Programmed Instruction in Medical Education,* Rochester, New York: The University of Rochester, 1965.

———, *Programmed Learning: Evolving Principles and Industrial Applications,* Ann Arbor, Mich.: Foundation for Research on Human Behavior, 1961.

———, and Hilliard Jason (Eds.), *Self-Instruction in Medical Education,* Rochester, N. Y.: The University of Rochester, 1966.

Mager, Robert F., *Preparing Objectives for Programmed Instruction,* San Francisco: Fearon, 1961.

Margulies, Stuart, and Lewis D. Eigen (Eds.), *Applied Programed Instruction,* New York: John Wiley and Sons, 1962.

Markle, Susan M., Lewis D. Eigen, and P. Kenneth Komoski, *A Programed Primer on Programing,* New York: The Center for Programed Instruction, 1961.

———, *Good Frames and Bad,* New York: John Wiley and Sons, 1964.

Newer Educational Media, papers of the Regional Research Conference, The Pennsylvania State University in cooperation with the U.S. Department of Health, Education, and Welfare, 1961.

New Teaching Aids for the American Classroom—A Symposium, The Institute for Communication Research, Stanford University, 1960.

Noll, Victor H., *Introduction to Educational Measurement,* Boston: Houghton Mifflin, 1957.

Nunney, Derek N. (Ed.), *New Approaches in Educational and Training Systems,* Detroit: Wayne State University, 1965. (Offset)

Ofiesh, Gabriel D., *Programmed Instruction: A Guide to Management,* New York: American Management Association, 1965.

———, and Wesley C. Meierhenry, *Trends in Programmed Instruction,* Washington, D.C.: National Education Association, 1964.

Pipe, Peter, *Practical Programming,* New York: Holt, Rinehart and

Winston, 1965.

Prescott, Daniel A., *The Child in the Education Process,* New York: McGraw-Hill, 1957.

Pressey, Sidney L., Francis P. Robinson, and John E. Horrocks, *Psychology in Education,* New York: Harper, 1959.

Roucek, Joseph S., *Programmed Teaching: A Symposium of Automation in Education,* New York: Philosophical Library, 1965.

Rutherford, Gladys (Ed.), *Programmed Learning—And Its Future in Canada,* report of a seminar held by the Canadian Teachers' Federation, 1961.

Schramm, Wilbur (Ed.), *The Research on Programmed Instruction,* Washington, D.C.: Office of Education, 1964 (OE-34034).

Smith, B. Othanel, William O. Stanley, and J. Harlan Shores, *Fundamentals of Curriculum Development,* revised edition, New York: World Book, 1957.

Smith, Wendell I., and J. William Moore, *Programmed Learning,* New York: Van Nostrand, 1962.

Stolurow, Laurence M., *Teaching by Machine* (OE-34010) Cooperative Research Monograph No. 6, Washington, D.C.: U.S. Government Printing Office, 1961.

Stroud, Jes B., *Psychology in Education,* New York: Longmans, Green, 1956.

Taber, Julian I., Robert Glaser, and Halmuth H. Schaefer, *Learning and Programmed Instruction,* Reading, Mass.: Addison-Wesley, 1965.

Teal, Gilbert (Ed.), *Programmed Instruction in Industry and Education,* Stamford, Conn.: Public Service Research, 1963.

Thomas, C. A., I. K. Davies, D. Openshaw, and J. B. Bird, *Programmed Learning in Perspective,* Chicago: Educational Methods, 1964.

Thomas, R. Murray, *Judging Student Progress,* New York: Longmans, Green, 1960.

Tyler, Ralph, *Basic Principles of Curriculum and Instruction,* Syllabus for Education 360, Chicago: The University of Chicago Press, 1950.

Varty, J., *Collegiate Programmed Instruction* (mimeo.), New York Brooklyn College.

Walther, R. E., and N. A. Crowder, *Techniques in Intrinsic Programming,* Silver Spring, Md.: U.S. Industries, Inc., 1965.

Wandt, Edwin, and Gerald W. Brown, *Essentials of Educational Evaluation,* New York: Henry Holt, 1957.

B. BIBLIOGRAPHICAL MATERIALS

Note: Many of the books listed in A contain valuable bibliographies, particularly Lumsdaine and Glaser, Lysaught, and Stolurow.

AID: *Auto-Instructional Devices for Education and Learning*; Institute of International Research and Development, Lubbock, Texas.

(This monthly magazine, now titled the *Journal of the National Society for Programmed Instruction,* publishes a running bibliography of articles, research reports, and publications.)

Campbell, Ina, *Teaching Machines and Programed Learning: A Bibliography,* New York: Teaching Materials Corp., 1961.

Finn, James D., and Donald G. Perrin, *Teaching Machines and Programmed Learning, 1962: A Survey of the Industry,* Occasional Paper No. 3, Washington, D.C.: National Education Association, 1962.

Fry, Edward B., Glenn L. Bryan, and Joseph W. Rigney, "Teaching Machines: An Annotated Bibliography," *Aud.-Vis. Comm. Rev.,* Vol. 8, No. 2, Supp. 1, Washington, D.C.: NEA Department of Audio-Visual Instruction, 1960.

Hendershot, C. H. (Ed.), *Programmed Learning: A Bibliography of Programs and Presentation Devices* (Offset), University Center, Michigan: Delta College (Quarterly).

Leavitt, Jerome E., and Rilla J. Edgar, *Programed Learning and Teaching Machines,* Instructional Services Section, State Department of Education, Salem, Oregon, 1961.

Lysaught, Jerome P., and Clarence M. Williams, *Bibliography on Programmed Learning: Publications, Programs and Devices,* Office of Educational Research, University of Rochester, 1962.

Programmed Instruction Materials Guide, 1964–1965, Institute of Educational Technology, New York: Teachers College Press, 1965.

Programs '62—A Guide to Programmed Instructional Materials Available to Educators by September 1962, The Center for Programed Instruction, New York, in cooperation with the U.S. Department of Health, Education, and Welfare, Washington, D.C.: U.S. Government Printing Office, 1962.

Rigney, Joseph W., and Edward B. Fry, *Current Teaching-Machine Programs and Programming Techniques, Aud-Vis. Comm. Rev.,* Vol. 9, No. 3, Supp. 3, Washington, D.C.: NEA Department of Audio-Visual Instruction, 1961.

Ross, Wilbur R., et al., *Teaching Machines: Industry Survey and Buyers' Guide,* New York: Center for Programed Instruction, 1962.

Varty, J., *Collegiate Programmed Instruction* (mimeo.), New York Brooklyn College.

C. JOURNALS AND PERIODICALS

Audiovisual Instruction, Washington, D.C.: Department of Audio-Visual Instruction, National Education Association.

Audio-Visual Communication Review, Department of Audio-Visual Instruction, National Education Association, Washington, D.C.

Contemporary Psychology, American Psychological Association, Washington, D.C.

Journal of the National Society for Programmed Instruction, San Antonio, Texas: NSPI, Trinity University.

Journal of Programed Instruction, The Center for Programed Instruction, Inc., New York City.

Programed Instruction, Newsletter, Center for Programed Instruction, Inc., New York City.

Teaching Aids News (now known as *Educational Technology*), Saddle Brook, N. J.: Educational News Service.

D. GENERAL ARTICLES OF A NON-TECHNICAL NATURE

Boehm, George A. W., "Can People Be Taught Like Pigeons?" *Fortune,* October, 1960.

Boroff, David, "The Three R's and Pushbuttons," *New York Times Magazine,* September 25, 1960.

Braley, Ian, "Will Robots Teach Your Child?" *Today's Living,* September 4, 1960.

Luce, G. G., "Can Machines Replace Teachers?" *Saturday Evening Post,* September 24, 1960.

Price, George R., "The Teaching Machine," *Think,* March, 1959.

E. PAPERS AND ARTICLES

Note: This listing is limited to those citations of particular import for this publication. The sources listed under A and B of this bibliography will provide an exhaustive compilation of the many papers and articles published on programmed learning and teaching machines.

Alexander, Howard, and R. F. Smith, "A Self-Instructional Program in Elementary Statistics," Earlham College, 1961, mimeo.

Allen, Layman E., "Progress Report of the All Project," Yale University, October 15, 1961, mimeo.

Angell, G. W., "The Effect of Immediate Knowledge of Quiz Results on Final Examination Scores in Freshman Chemistry," *Journ. of Educ. Res.,* **42**:391–94, January, 1949.

———, and M. E. Troyer, "A New Self-Scoring Test Device for Improving Instruction," *School and Society,* **67**:84–5, January 31, 1948 (Lumsdaine and Glaser, pp. 66–68).

Banghart, Frank W., "An Experiment with Teaching Machines and Programmed Textbooks," University of Virginia, undated, mimeo.

Barlow, John A., "Conversational Chaining in Teaching Machine Programs," Earlham College, 1960, mimeo. (See also the article by the same title in *Psychol. Rep.,* **8**:207–209, 1960.)

———, "The Earlham College Self-Instructional Program," *Aud.-Vis.*

Comm. Rev., Vol. 8, 1960, pp. 207–209.

Barlow, John A., "Earlham College Student Self-Instructional Project, First Quarterly Report." Earlham College, 1959, mimeo. (Lumsdaine and Glaser, pp. 416–21).

Benson, Eugene, and Felix Kopstein, "Machine Teaching of Basic Electronics at Keesler Air Force Base: An Experiment and Results," paper delivered at the NEA Department of Audio-Visual Instruction convention in Miami, Florida, April 24, 1961.

Blyth, John W., "Teaching Machines and Human Beings," *The Educ. Rec.,* April, 1960 (Lumsdaine and Glaser, pp. 401–415).

Briggs, L. J., "The Development and Appraisal of Special Procedures for Superior Students and an Analysis of the Effects of 'Knowledge of Results.'" *Ohio State University Abstracts of Dissertations, 1948–49,* Columbus: Ohio State University, 1950.

Coulson, John E., and Harry F. Silberman, "Effects of Three Variables in a Teaching Machine," *Journ. of Educ. Psych.,* **51**:135–43, June, 1960.

Craytor, J. K. and J. P. Lysaught, "Programmed Instruction in Nursing Education: A Trial Use," *Nursing Research,* Vol. 13, No. 4, Fall, 1964.

Crowder, Norman A., "Automatic Tutoring by Intrinsic Programming," 1960 (Lumsdaine and Glaser, pp. 286–98).

———, "A Sample Sequence from the Tutortext on The Arithmetic of Computers," Goleta, Calif.: United States Industries, Inc., 1960.

Eigen, Lewis D., "The Construction of Frames of an Automated Teaching Program," revised, New York: Center for Programed Instruction, 1960, mimeo.

———, "Some Problems in Field Testing Programs for Teaching Machines," *Journ. of Educ. Soc.,* Vol. 34, No. 8: 372–6, 1961.

———, and P. Kenneth Komoski, "Automated Teaching Project, Collegiate School," New York: Center for Programed Instruction, 1960, mimeo.

———, "Research Summary No. 1 of the Collegiate School Automatic Teaching Project," New York: Center for Programed Instruction, 1960, mimeo.

Evans, J. L., R. Glaser, and L. Homme, "The RULEG System for the Construction of Programmed Verbal Learning Sequences," Project No. 691 (9417), University of Pittsburgh, 1960.

Finn, J. D., "Technology and the Instructional Process," *Phi Delta Kappan,* XLI:9:371–78, June, 1960.

Flory, John, and Thomas W. Hope, "Non-Theatrical Films–Interim Report No. 2," *Journ. of the SMPTE,* Vol. 70, January, 1961.

Fry, Edward B., "A Study of Teaching Machine Response Modes," 1960 (Lumsdaine and Glaser, pp. 469–74).

Geis, George L., "Program Preparation," Stamford, Conn.: Public Service Research, Inc., 1961, mimeo.

Gilbert, Thomas F., "An Early Approximation to Principles of Programming Continuous Discourse, Self-Instructional Materials," Bell Telephone Laboratories, September, 1958, mimeo. (A summary of this report is contained in Lumsdaine and Glaser, pp. 630–34.)

Gilbert, Thomas F., "Mathematics: The Technology of Education, I. The General System," New York: TOR Education, Inc., 1961, mimeo.

Holland, James G., "Programming Verbal Knowledge," Harvard Psychological Laboratories, 1960, mimeo.

———, "A Teaching Machine Program in Psychology," 1959 (Galanter, pp. 69–82).

———, "Teaching Machines: An Application of Principles from the Laboratory," 1960 (Lumsdaine and Glaser, pp. 215–28).

"IBM 709 Tutors M.I.T. Students," *AID,* November, 1961, p. 67.

"Implementation Studies," *Programed Instruction,* Vol. 1, No. 4, February, 1962, p. 3.

"Iowa Every-Pupil Test of Basic Skills," new edition, 1940–50. Boston: Houghton Mifflin.

Jensen, B. T., "An Independent-Study Laboratory Using Self-Scoring Tests," *Journ. of Educ. Res.,* 43:134–37, October, 1949.

Klaus, David J., "The Art of Auto-Instructional Programming." A.I.R. Memorandum No. 15, Pittsburgh, Pa.: American Institute for Research, 1960, mimeo.

———, "Some Observations and Findings from Auto-Instructional Research," Pittsburgh, Pa.: American Institute for Research, 1960, mimeo.

Komoski, P. Kenneth, "Programming by Teachers for the School Curriculum," New York: Center for Programed Instruction, 1961, mimeo.

Krumboltz, John D., "Meaningful Learning and Retention: Practice and Reinforcement Variables," *Rev. of Educ. Res.,* Vol. XXXI, No. 5, December, 1961, pp. 535–546.

———, and Ronald Weisman, "The Effect of Overt vs. Covert Responding to Programed Material," *Journ. of Educ. Psych.,* April, 1962.

Little, J. K., "Results of Use of Machines for Testing and for Drill upon Learning in Educational Psychology," *Journ. of Exp. Educ.,* 3:45–49, September, 1934 (Lumsdaine and Glaser, pp. 59–65).

Lysaught, Jerome P., "A Commentary on the State of the Art," *AID,* November, 1961.

———, "Industrial Training Through Programmed Learning," *Personnel Journ.,* September, 1961.

———, "Programmed Learning and the Classroom Teacher," *New York State Education,* February, 1961.

———, "Programmed Learning and Teaching Machines in Industrial Training," Parts I and II, *Journ. of the Am. Soc. of Training Dir.,* February and June, 1961.

———, "An Analysis of Factors Related to Success in Constructing Programmed Learning Sequences," *Journal of Programmed Instruction,* Vol. 2, No. 3, Fall, 1963.

Lysaught, Jerome P., "Telling the Staff About Programmed Learning," *Overview,* Vol. 3, No. 11, November, 1962.

———, "A Survey of Industrial Training-for-Trainers," *Training Directors Journal,* Vol. 18, No. 1, January, 1964.

———, "Programmed Instruction: A New Departure in Medical Education," *The New Physician,* Vol. 13, No. 4, April, 1964.

———, "Self-Instructional Medical Programs: A Survey," *The New Physician,* Vol. 13, No. 5, May, 1964.

———, "Selecting Instructional Programmers," *Training Directors Journal,* Vol. 18, No. 6, June, 1964.

———, "Selecting Auto-Instructional Programmers," *Personnel Journal,* Vol. 43, No. 7, July–August, 1964.

———, "A Prediction of Success Among Auto-Instructional Programmers," *Journal of the National Society for Programmed Instruction,* Vol. 3, No. 7, September, 1964. Jointly Published in *Teaching Aids News,* Vol. 4, No. 19, October, 1964.

———, "An Analysis of Four Years' Experience in Development Instructional Programmers," *Teaching Aids News,* Vol. 4, No. 24, December, 1964.

———, "Programming and the Teacher," *New York State Education,* Vol. 52, No. 4, January, 1965. Reprinted in *Canadian School Journal,* Vol. 43, No. 3, April, 1965.

———, "Learner Reactions to a Large Scale Use of Programmed Instruction for Medical Education," *The New Physician,* Vol. 14, No. 6, June, 1965.

———, "Self-Instructional Programs in Continuing Education," *Medical Times,* Vol. 93, No. 9, September, 1965.

———, "Predictions of Success Among Programers and Implications for Industrial Training." In Nunney, D. N. (Ed.), *New Approaches in Training and Educational Systems,* Detroit: Wayne State University, 1965 (offset).

———, "Das Erarbeiten von Lehrprogrammen—boobachtete Ruckwirkungen auf den Lehrer," *Deutsche Lehrprogramme fur Schule und Praxis,* No. 3, June, 1965.

———, "Instructional Changes Among Teachers Trained in Programing," *Teaching Aids News,* Vol. 5, No. 17. September, 1965.

———, "Programmed Instruction and the Industrial Arts," Proceedings of the Summer School Graduate Conference in Industrial Arts Education. State University College, Oswego, New York. October, 1965 (offset).

———, "Report on an Advanced Course in Programing Materials for Self-Instruction," *Teaching Aids News,* Vol. 5, No. 22, November, 1965.

———, "Inducing Classroom Change Through Programer Training," *Programed Instruction,* Vol. 5, No. 1. October, 1965.

———, and Hilliard Jason. "Programmed Instruction in Medical Education: Report of the Rochester Conference," *Journal of Medical Education,* Vol. 40, No. 5, May, 1965.

Lysaught, Jerome P., and Clarence M. Williams, "A Community Explores Programmed Learning," Parts I and II, *New York State Education,* February and March, 1962.

———, ———, "Programmed Learning at All Levels," *New York State Education,* Vol. 49, No. 6, March, 1962.

———, C. D. Sherman, Jr., and C. M. Williams, "A Feasibility Study: Programmed Instruction in Medical Education," *Journal of the National Society for Programmed Instruction,* Vol. 2, No. 8, October, 1963. (Abstract)

———, ———, ———, "Medical Schools and Programmed Instruction," *Spectrum,* Vol. 11, No. 4, November–December, 1963.

———, ———, ———, "Utilization of Programmed Instruction in Medical Education," *Journal of Medical Education,* Vol. 39, No. 8, August, 1964.

———, ———, ———, "Programmed Learning: Potential Values for Medical Instruction," *Journal of the American Medical Association,* Vol. 189, No. 11, September, 1964.

Mayer, Sylvia R., "Use of a Teaching Machine for Air Force On-the-job Training in the SAGE System," Air Force Command and Control Development Division, Report No. AFCCDD-TN-60-51, 1960.

McNamara, W. J., and John L. Hughes, "IBM's Experience in Developing Programmed Instruction," in Lysaught, Jerome P. (Ed.), *Programmed Learning: Evolving Principles and Industrial Applications,* Ann Arbor, Mich.: Foundation for Research on Human Behavior, 1961.

Mellan, Ibert, "Teaching and Educational Inventions," *Journ. of Exp. Educ.,* **4**:291–300, March, 1936 (Lumsdaine and Glaser, pp. 265–74).

Peterson, J. C., "A New Device for Teaching, Testing, and Research in Learning," *Trans. of the Kan. Acad. of Sci.,* **33**:41–47, 1930.

Porter, Douglas, "A Critical Review of a Portion of the Literature on Teaching Devices," *Harvard Educ. Rev.,* **27**:126–47, Spring, 1957 (Lumsdaine and Glaser, pp. 114–132).

———, "Some Effects of Year Long Teaching Machine Instruction," 1959 (Galanter, pp. 85–90).

———, "Teaching Machines," *Harvard Grad. Sch. of Educ. Assn. Bull.,* **3**:1–5, March, 1958 (Lumsdaine and Glaser, pp. 206–14).

Pressey, S. L., "Basic Unresolved Teaching-Machine Problems," *Theory into Practice,* Vol. 1, No. 1, February, 1962, Bureau of Educational Research and Services, Ohio State University, Columbus.

———, "A Simple Apparatus Which Gives Tests and Scores—and Teaches," *School and Society,* **23**:373–376, March, 1926 (Lumsdaine and Glaser, pp. 35–41).

———, "A Third and Fourth Contribution Toward the Coming Industrial Revolution in Education," *School and Society,* **36**:668–672,

November, 1932 (Lumsdaine and Glaser, pp. 47–51).

Pressey, S. L., "Development and Appraisal of Devices Providing Immediate Automatic Scoring of Objective Tests and Concomitant Self-Instruction," *Journ. of Psych.*, **29**:417–447, April, 1950 (Lumsdaine and Glaser, pp. 69–88).

Quackenbush, Jack, "How Effective Are the New Auto-Instructional Materials and Devices?" *IRE Trans. on Educ.*, **4**:144–151, December, 1961.

Rath, Gustave, N. S. Andersen, and R. C. Brainerd, "The IBM Research Center Teaching Machine Project," 1959 (Galanter, pp. 117–130).

Roe, Arnold, et al., "Automated Teaching Methods Using Linear Programs," Report Nos. 60–53 and 60–105, Automated Learning Research Project, University of California, Department of Engineering.

Rothkopf, Ernst Z., "A Suggested 'Label' for Self-Instructional Programs," *Aud.-Vis. Comm. Rev.*, January–February, 1962.

Rushton, E. W., "Programmed Learning in the Roanoke, Virginia, City School System," January, 1961, mimeo. (See also the author's article "The Roanoke Experiment," *Nation's Schools*, **67**:76–79, February, 1961.)

Skinner, B. F., "The Science of Learning and the Art of Teaching," *Harvard Educ. Rev.*, **24**:86–97, Spring, 1954 (Lumsdaine and Glaser, pp. 99–113).

———, "Why We Need Teaching Machines," New York: Appleton-Century-Crofts, 1961. (Reprint from B. F. Skinner, *Cumulative Record*, enlarged edition, New York: Appleton-Century-Crofts, 1961, pp. 182.04–5.)

Smith, D. E. P., "Speculations: Characteristics of Successful Programs and Programmers," 1959 (Galanter, pp. 91–102).

Smith, Wendell, and J. W. Moore, "Size-of-Step and Achievement in Programmed Spelling," Bucknell University, 1961, mimeo. (Reprinted in Smith and Moore, *Programmed Learning*, New York: Van Nostrand, 1962.)

"TEMAC Programmed Learning Materials, Report No. 2," Wilmette, Ill.: Encyclopaedia Britannica Films, April, 1961.

Van Atta, Loche, "Research Notes," *Automated Teaching Bull.*, Vol. 1, No. 2, December, 1959.

Weaver, David O., "Suggested Techniques in Preparing Programmed Learning: the Elements of 'How to' for Linear Programming," *Journ. of the Am. Soc. of Training Dir.*, May, 1961.

F. FILMS, FILMSTRIPS, AND TAPES *

Basic Skill Films, two filmstrips, 62 frames, color: *Teaching Machines* and *An Example of a Teaching Machine Program*.

Carousel Films, *Learning and Behavior* (Charles Collingwood interviews B. F. Skinner), 16 mm sound, b&w, 30 min.

National Education Association, Department of Audio-Visual Instruction, *Programmed Instructional Materials for Use in Teaching Machines,* magnetic tape recording, 90 min.

National Education Association, Department of Audio-Visual Instruction, *Teaching Machines and Programmed Learning* (Skinner, Lumsdaine, and Glaser), 16 mm sound, b&w, 28 min.

Rheem Califone Corporation, two films on teaching machines: (1) Evan Keislar and Sidney Pressey; (2) Art Linkletter and guests; 16 mm sound, b&w, kinescope.

University of Washington, Audio-Visual Services, *Teaching Machines, Parts I and II,* 16 mm sound, b&w, 30 min. each.

Videosonics Division, Hughes Aircraft Corporation, *Man-Machine Techniques for Education and Training Systems,* 16 mm sound, b&w, 30 min.

* Means and procedures for obtaining these materials can be found in an audio-visual center, directory, or library.

Index

Ability, student, 43
Achievement, student, 44
Amsel, A., 132
Assumptions, 17
  about learners, 42 ff.
Audio-visual aids, 19
Auto-instructional devices, 2, 160 ff.
Auto-instructional methods, 2

Background, student, 47 f.
Barlow, J., 42, 73–76, 91, 153
Bartz, A. E., 50
Beck, J., 91
Behavioral outcomes, 54
  of instruction, 144
Bloom, B. S., 69, 146
Blyth, J. W., 13, 166
Bolles, R. C., 27
Briggs, L. J., 166
Broudy, H., 154
Brown, G. W., 147

Carr, W. J., 27
Center for Programed Instruction, The, 41, 133, 167
Conditioned reinforcers, 6
Cook, D., 28
Coulson, J. E., 166
Cram, D., 26
Crowder, N., 81 f., 87, 88, 91
Cueing, 110 ff.
  and fading, 126 f.
  logical, 112 ff.
Curriculum, effects of programs on, 157 f.

Dale, E., 69
Diagnostic test, example, 46
Differential reinforcement, 7

Editing, 119 ff.
  accuracy and relevance, 120 f.
  style and vocabulary, 121 f.
Eigen, L. D., 28, 117, 118, 167
Error analysis, 135 ff.
Evaluation, 134 ff.
  constant, 18
Experiments, design of, 144 ff.
Extinguishing, 8

Feedback, immediate, 18
Ferster, C. B., 166
Field testing, immediate, 122 ff.
Finn, J. D., 41, 166
Foley, A., 153
Foltz, C. I., 167
Frames, criterion, 79 ff.; *see also* Items
French, W., 69

Fry, E. B., 41, 91
Fullagar, W., 16
Furst, E. J., 146

Gagne, R. M., 27
Galanter, E. H., 26, 27, 91, 117, 132, 166
Geis, G., 100, 101
Gilbert, T. F., 95, 97, 117
Glaser, R., 27, 91, 118, 132, 133, 166
Goldberg, I. A., 28
Gotkin, L., 146
Guest, L., 50

Hilgard, E. R., 27
Holland, J. G., 6, 13, 27, 91, 99, 100, 118, 132, 146
Homme, L. E., 118
Horrocks, J. E., 51
Hughes, J. L., 167

Industrial use, 39 f.
Intelligence, student, 43
Items, 8 ff.
  components of, checking and instruction, 114 f.
    information, 105 ff.
    other considerations, 116 f.
    response, 109 ff.
  construction of, 102 ff.
    exceptions to, 104 f.
  defective, 128 f.
  definition of, 102
  forcing, 105
  ordering of, 92 ff.
  typical, 9
  use of, 102 f.
    delayed repetition, 116
    generalization, 116
    interlocking, 116
    restatement, 116
    review, 116
    rote review, 116
    specification, 116
    terminating, 116 f.

Kearney, N. C., 69
Keislar, E. R., 166
Keller, F. S., 27
Kendler, H. H., 27
Klaus, D. J., 100, 132, 167
Knight, W. J., 167
Komoski, P. K., 100
Krauss, R., 53

Ladder of abstraction, 54 ff.
Learner, role of, 155 ff.
Levine, S. L., 167
Lindgren, H. C., 50
Little, J. K., 12
Lumsdaine, A. A., 27, 70, 91, 118, 132, 166, 167
Lysaught, J. P., 91, 167

Mager, R. F., 69
Margulies, S., 28, 118, 167
Markle, S. M., 28
Mathetics system, 95 ff.
Mechner, F., 28
Mellan, I., 166
Meno, 3 ff.
Meyer, S. R., 132
Model, selection of, 70
  program, differences in, 86 f.
Motivational effects, 7

Noll, V. A., 147

Objectives, 17
  constructing, 52 ff.
  immediate, 53
  samples of, 60 ff.
  taxonomy of, 58 f.
  ultimate, 53
Operational definitions, 53
Ordering of items, 61, 92 ff.
  mathetics, 95 ff.
  other approaches, 97 ff.
  pragmatic, 93 f.
  RULEG, 94 f.

Panels, 60, 103
Paradigms, effects of, 88 f.
  selection of, 70 ff.
Pennington, D. F., 118
Perrin, D. G., 41, 166
Porter, D., 12, 166

Pragmatic ordering, 93 f.
Prescott, D. A., 50
Pressey, S. L., 5, 27, 51, 151
Program, administration of, 151
conversational chaining, 73 ff.
learning, 2
Programmed instruction, application of, 148 ff.
complementation, 150
enrichment, 150
remediation, 151
review, 151
Programmed learning, characteristics of, 16 ff.
misconceptions of, 19 ff.
Programmed sequence, 9
Programming, definition of, 2
effects on teachers, 23, 153 ff.
process of, 23 ff.
state of the art of, 159 f.
Programs, construction of, 92 ff.
effects of, on curriculum, 157 f.
on learner, 155 ff.
on teacher, 153 ff.
extrinsic, 71 ff.
full branching, 87 f.
information to accompany, 141 ff.
intrinsic, 81 ff.
linear, 71 ff.
linear with criterion frames, 79 ff.
linear with sub-linears, 78 f.
modified linear, 76 ff.
use of, 21 ff., 149 ff.
Prompting, *see* Cueing
Purpose, student, 48 f.

Quackenbush, J., 155, 156, 157, 167

Ramo, S., 166
Rate, individual, 18
Reading level, student, 45
Reinforcement, 6
Reinforcement theory, 6, 7, 8
and classroom practice, 8
generalizations from, 7
Reinforcers, 6
Research, generalizations from, 15, 16
Responding, active, 17
Response, 9
arranging for student, 109 ff.
constructed, 86
multiple choice, 86
Response sheet, student, 123 f.
Review of sequence, 119 ff.
ambiguity, 126
cueing and fading, 126 f.
errors and error level, 124 f.
further considerations, 127 f.
item difficulty, 125 f.
item length, 125
rewriting, 124 ff.
Rigney, J. W., 41
Roanoke experiment, 1, 149 f.
Robinson, F. P., 51
Rothkopf, E. F., 141, 144
RULEG system, 94 f.

Sapon, S. M., 166
Selection of a unit, 29 ff.
criteria for, 30 ff.
depressed level of learning, 34 ff.
ease of treatment, 31 ff.
field of study, 30 f.
length, 33 f.
logical order of material, 36 f.
special student needs, 37 ff.
Sequence, logical, 17
Shaping, 6, 7
Shores, H. J., 41
Silvern, L. C., 167
Skinner, B. F., 6, 13, 27, 81, 91, 118
Skipping, item(s), 77
Slack, C. W., 118
Small steps, 17
Smith, B. O., 41
Smith, D. E. P., 100, 117
Socratic method, 3 ff.
Stanley, W. O., 41
Stimulus, 9
information component of, 105 ff.
Stimulus-response theories, 9 ff.
Stolurow, L., 28, 161
Stroud, J. B., 51

Teacher, role of, 21, 153 ff.
Teacher ratings, 45

Teaching machines, 2, 5, 160 ff.
  as research tool, 164 ff.
  desirability of, 163 f.
  necessity of, 162 f.
Test, construction of, 137 ff.
  diagnostic, 45
  program is not a, 20
  two-way chart, 138 ff.
Testing, 134
  diagnostic, 137 ff.
  post-test, 140 f.
  pre-test data, 137 ff.
Thomas, R. M., 147
Thorndike, E. L., 9
Tracks, program, 80
Tutorial method, 3
Tyler, R., 41

Unit, selection of, 29 ff.

Wandt, E., 147
Weaver, D. O., 118

Zeaman, D., 27